VIGILANTE
HANDBOOK

By
VICTOR
SANTORO

 DESERT PUBLICATIONS

VIGILANTE HANDBOOK
by Victor Santoro

© 1981

Desert Publications

ISBN: 0-87947-445-9

DESERT PUBLICATIONS
Cornville, Arizona 86325

Table of Contents

This book is dedicated to hard-core realism, which most people tend to ignore.

Introduction

This is a practical book on what vigilantism is today, and the emphasis is on the nuts and bolts of vigilantism. I will cover the history briefly, and touch upon the theory, but as most people are interested in the here and now rather than the past and the remote, most of the attention will focus on who present-day vigilantes are, why they are, how they go about it, and how successful they are.

This is bound to be a controversial book because it will bring up some unpopular ideas that are sure to offend a number of people, such as the notion that self-defense is a legitimate aim and that vigilantism is a desireable thing when there is no good alternative.

Citizens of other countries may look down on us for our practice of vigilantism but in fact few of them have any reason to feel superior. Indeed, other countries have or have had their vigilante or quasi-vigilante organizations. To name a few:

France: The Committe of Public Safety, 1798.
         The Milice, 1941-44
         The Resistance, 1941-45
         The OAS, Secret Army Organization, 1960-65, app.
Brazil: Police Death Squads, during the past couple of decades.

This is a sketchy listing, and only a tiny part of the organizations that have existed for vigilante, quasi-vigilante, and pseudo-vigilante purposes in recent history. Most of these have existed more for political purposes than to fight crime.

1

VIGILANTE HANDBOOK

American vigilantes are usually not political but rather directly oriented toward fighting crime. There have been some conspicuous exceptions, however, and the fact that these too have been labeled "vigilantes" has tended to give vigilantes a bad name.

Traditionally, vigilantism is a direct response by the citizens to a serious crime problem that has gotten out of hand. When formal law and order are weak, inefficient, overwhelmed, corrupt, or just do not exist, then the citizens enforce the law directly.

On the frontier, where sheriffs, marshals, courts and judges were few and far between, vigilantism was common. It happened many more times than are recorded that the citizens enforced the laws themselves, without fanfare and in the most direct and summary manner possible.

History only records the formal "Committee of Vigilance", "Posse Comitatus", and "Regulator" organization. The countless instances of cattle rustlers or highwaymen shot summarily and buried out on the prairie are lost to history. We will never know how many times it happened that a felon received "frontier justice" and was quietly interred without further ado. The citizens had to get on with the day-to-day business of eking a living out of frontier conditions: they had no time to keep detailed records.

Today some of the same conditions exist. We have formally constituted police and courts but they cannot be everywhere at once. People do take it upon themselves to enforce the laws when they are forced either to do so or to succumb to the criminals.

Vigilantism does not belong only to the past: it is part of the present and it is definitely in our future.

This book is organized into two major sections:

Part One deals with what some people would call theory; the history of vigilantism, causes of crime, the breakdown of society's traditional methods of defense, etc.

Part Two is concerned with the nuts and bolts of vigilantism today. It is the practical section, with chapters on what is being done, who is doing it, and how it is being done. The emphasis is on tactics and techniques.

PART I.
VIGILANTISM IN PERSPECTIVE

1. Who Is The Criminal?

When dealing with as broad a subject as crime it is important, for the sake of practicality, to narrow down the field of discussion as quickly as possible and to focus immediately on the specific problem.

Because of the great number of laws and the various means of enforcing them, there is a great number and variety of lawbreakers. We have all, at one time or another in our lives, broken some law or laws. This makes us lawbreakers but, as we shall see, not criminals. Some ways to run afoul of the law are:

a) Carelessness or error. Most traffic offenses fall into this category, as does spitting on the sidewalk, leaving your dog off the leash, etc. These are petty offenses and need not concern us further.

b) Mental disturbances. Kleptomaniacs and compulsive arsonists fall into this category, as do child killers and the perpetrators of other "atrocity" crimes. These are truly sick people and usually the police can cope with them better than vigilantes can.

c) "Doin' what comes naturally" is at the root of many instances of lawbreaking, such as 2nd and 3rd degree rape. Many teen-agers break the law by having sexual relations with a female who is under the age of consent, even though she may be of the same age as they, and run afoul of a law that was designed to protect juveniles against adult degenerates.

d) "Crimes of passion". These are acts of anger, such as the murder or beating arising out of a lovers' triangle, or the 2nd degree murder that results from a drunken argument between friends. These, like the above crimes, are in the category of casual or accidental crimes, and usually not committed by hardened lawbreakers.

5

e) Crime for profit. This is the hard core of crime committed by people who know what they do and enjoy doing it, and indeed make a living at it. Crime for profit covers everything from petty chiseling to price-fixing, through embezzlement and burglary, and ending up with robbery and murder for profit. This area is where the career criminals are to be found, the recidivists who serve their prison sentences if and when they are caught and go out and resume their interrupted careers upon release.

These are the people who frustrate the social workers, policemen, legislators and do-gooders because they are so resistant to change. They steadfastly refuse to "go straight". This is the category which, according to experienced policemen, provide 85% of the street crime statistics.

These are the repeat offenders. While some others may occasionally commit a crime for profit they are amateurs and easily separated from the career criminals by the fact that they do not continue in crime as a way of life.

2. The "Causes Of Crime"

Sociologists, psychologists, clergymen and politicians all have their theories as to the "causes of crime". They often contradict each other and in the long run contribute little toward either understanding crime or solving the problem. A quick look at some of the theories will establish the atmosphere:

a) Psychological causes. A psychologist will tell you that criminals are the way they are because of something in their pasts, an unhappy childhood. This is very interesting to hear but in fact many of us have had unhappy childhoods without growing up to be criminals. An unhappy childhood is not a license to kill, or to rob, for that matter. This explanation is very unsatisfying.

b) Socio-economic causes. Sociologists and penologists say that crime is due to socio-economic causes; the poor steal to eat and then they go on to greater things. They point out that crime allegedly increases during periods of economic stress, such as depression or recession. This explanation neglects the fact that the well-to-do steal too, and that many of the most successful criminals are not living hand-to-mouth, stealing only the crust of bread that they eat, but are living in a lavish lifestyle from the proceeds of their crimes.

Big crime actually begets bigger crime, and the biggest criminals of all seem never to be satisfied but are constantly seeking to expand their criminal domains.

c) The "breakdown" of religion and mores. According to this theory the current decline in religious observance is at the root of crime, as people lose the sense of right and wrong that they would get from religion. This theory ignores the fact that throughout the ages there have been many people who were not active church-goers. There has also been no evidence to show that atheists are more prone to become criminals than others. Additionally, some noted organized crime figures are strong believers.

d) Decline of public confidence in "law and order". The massive evidence shown in recent years of public figures flouting the law and getting away with it has sapped people's belief in the validity of right and wrong, according to this theory. When people see the biggest criminals of all getting away with it on the six o'clock news, it persuades them that there is no point in obeying the law.

While it is a fact that a number of our public figures, including a former president and many legislators, have been caught with their hands dirty, this is still a shotgun approach and does not explain why only some of the people in the country have taken to crime as a career.

e) Materialism. Some correctly point out that Americans are among the most materialistic people on earth and that this value system leads to greed and then to an attitude of acquisitiveness no matter what the means. Again, this is a shotgun approach. Not everybody raised in this materialistic society becomes a career criminal, just as not every ghetto resident becomes a mugger or drug addict.

The fact remains that we do not have any clear idea of the "causes" of crime. There are many theories that look good on paper but each one has gaps in it, none of them can be proven by any standard of evidence, and they tend to contradict each other.

More importantly, these theories are of little use in attacking the problem. It is nice to say that there would be less crime if people were not so greedy, but the fact is that people are and nobody has come up with a way to make people less greedy. Again, some will claim that the decline in religion is at the root of it all, but nobody can propose a concrete solution that will work in the real world. It would not be practical to force everyone to attend church.

If unhappy childhoods have anything to do with it, there is really no hope, as we cannot undo the past.

Crime is pretty much of an individual matter, and each of

us has to make his own choice as to whether he will earn his living by honest or dishonest means.

The central fact is that crime pays. It pays well and it always did. For those who have any doubt about the matter documentation will be found in a book titled "Crime Pays!" by Thomas Plate, (Simon & Schuster, 1975).

Despite many people's saying that "crime does not pay", it does. Some play numbers games, citing a case where a mugger got caught and sentenced to say, three years, with a "take" from his crime coming to say $50, and say that dividing the time spent in prison by the money stolen affords the mugger an income of less than two dollars a month and that "proves" that crime does not pay.

This is fallacious logic. Many criminals do not get caught and the smartest do not ever see the inside of a prison.

Some years back a national newsmagazine cited the results of a study which had found that the average intelligence quotient of prison inmates was about 85. This supposedly "proved" that criminals are stupid. The flaw in this logic is that the ones who were examined were the criminals who had gotten caught, convicted, and gotten prison sentences.

If somehow a study could be made of criminals who have not been caught it might turn out that they are smarter than the general population. Without a doubt, the biggest criminals of all are pretty intelligent, as they have shown considerable talent and ingenuity in circumventing the law. The picture, as fostered by some of the fictional representations, of the crime czar as a sullen and moronic hood more at home with a blackjack than with a book is just that— fiction.

In reality the dividing line between criminal pursuits and legitimate business is very hazy and it is very difficult to point out, much less define. Complicating the picture is that both fields require similar arrays of talents. A businessman who engages in price-fixing is not any stupider than his honest competitor. The merchant who knowingly buys "hot" goods to sell in his store may even by considered smarter. It can even be disputed that the "ethical" drug company that sells gelatin capsules to narcotics dealers are doing perfectly legitimate business, even though they know that the capsules will be used to package narcotics in quantities for retail sale.

3. Solving The Crime Problem - Traditional Approaches

Solving the crime "problem" really means solving several different problems. As there are many steps in the commission of a crime for profit, the process can be interdicted at various points along the way. This section will examine a few approaches that do work with varying effectiveness at various times. This is by no means an exhaustive listing, as that would take a book in itself. It is just a once-over of the common means that work most of the time.

a) Blocking opportunity for crime occurs when a business has a system of checks to detect and prevent employee theft, or when a motorist takes the keys out of his car when he leaves it. This does not stop the determined criminal but it will frustrate the casual thief.

b) Patrol, either by the police or by private security guards, has been shown to be effective in reducing the rate of street crime.

c) Deterrent. The severity of punishment and the risk of detection serve as deterrents to crime some of the time. The effect is lessened when the machinery for bringing this about is seen to be unreliable or ineffective, a complaint which is common among policemen today.

d) Imprisonment or probation serve to reduce crime by keeping the criminal "out of circulation" in the first instance and by close supervision of his activities in the second. Some people complain that prison sentences are too short and that some of those sentenced to probation should be locked up because they need closer supervision.

Physical custody does stop crime but in fact only a tiny percentage of criminals are in prison at any given moment, so its usefulness is limited.

e) Execution is the final solution, but unpopular these days. Whatever the merits of the arguments for capital punishment may be, the fact is that the criminal who is executed has his criminal career brought to a halt then and there.

Whatever the measures used, they are effective some of the time and do not work so well other times. In the best of societies, however, there are the few who, no matter how much material wealth they accumulate, are never satisfied and always want more. When this leads them to use any means, even if they are dishonest, we have crime, We try to keep it "down to a dull roar" but are not always successful. What happens when we fail is the subject of the next chapter.

4. Why Cops Can't Cope

At times the crime situation gets so severe that the police and the criminal justice system can no longer keep the "lid" on. To blame it all on "the kids", "soft-headed judges", or "liberals" is to oversimplify a complex problem. There are several reasons why the cops are sometimes less than effective in fighting what people perceive as a "crime wave".

First, we have to recognize that there are three kinds of crime for profit, which is our main concern here.

STREET CRIME is the unorganized actions by individuals or small bands, covering crimes such as burglary, mugging, robbery, some auto theft, vandalism, etc.

ORGANIZED CRIME is crime run by tightly organized groups of criminals, with a formal organization, literally a mini-government. Organized crime deals in larger projects, such as distributing contraband materials such as drugs, receiving and disposing of stolen goods such as automobiles, and the organization has sections which take care of what can be called the supportive services such as bribing public officials, defending the members who are arrested, transporting and smuggling goods, and enforcing its decrees.

WHITE COLLAR CRIME is non-violent crime practiced by people one would not normally categorize as criminals or "the criminal type". It includes check-forging, fraud and bunco, pricefixing, various sharp practices in otherwise legitimate businesses, embezzlement, etc. White collar crime is a special problem in its own right and in many ways it is the most difficult to fight.

Street crime usually responds to aggressive patrol, stakeouts, and stiff sentences. When the system breaks down, it is usually because of saturation. The police are overworked and they can't be everywhere at once.

During the first half of the Twentieth Century the police were winning the fight against street crime because they concentrated on the problem and attacked it with vigor. They made arrests and they made them stick. There were few enough criminals so that they could be "handled" and locked up. During the past few decades, though, the policeman's role has changed. Today people expect more from the police. People expect the police to find lost children, get a cat down from a tree, settle family fights, arbitrate neighborhood disputes, everything, in fact, except fighting crime. It is literally true that today policemen on patrol spend ninety five to ninety eight percent of their time in activities other than fighting crime. In every police department of more than a few men, there are always a few units concerned directly with fighting crime. These are the detectives, the anti-crime squads, the stakeout details, and a few others. They are the minority.

Saturation means that the police are busy doing other things as well as fighting crime, while the street crime problem gets to be too much to handle. The backlog of cases grows.

Additionally, in some neighborhoods the relationship between the police and the citizenry can be compared to that between an occupying army and the subject peoples. Policemen are repeatedly assaulted, sometimes killed. They cannot defend themselves, so they cannot defend the citizens.

Organized crime is more difficult to handle, even in the best of times. The "mobs" are too big, they overlap jurisdictions, their mobility makes them hard to keep under surveillance, and the manpower required to do the job is a drain on all, even the biggest police forces. Additionally, there are four factors that make coping with organized crime next to impossible:

a) Corruption. The "mob" greases palms. They buy cops, prosecutors, judges, and legislators. They have a huge amount of money and they spread it around bribing demoralized officials. It is true that money talks, and there is always a small number of policemen and others who are susceptible to bribery. That's all it takes, a small minority, to frustrate the efforts of the majority of honest policemen. Mobsters are kept informed of the police's activities, the progress of an investigation, tipped off to impending raids, evidence is "lost" or "misplaced", court cases are delayed endlessly, etc., etc.

A side effect of corruption is that the honest officials become demoralized. They start to feel that it is impossible to beat "the system", and that it is no longer worth trying. After a while, a mob can enjoy virtual immunity in a certain locale.

b) Compartmentalization. Modern organized crime is so big that it is broken up into different divisions, as are legitimate businesses. While each part is not quite autonomous and independent penetrating one or disabling another does not kill the whole organization. A police informer might tell all about the West Side numbers operation, for example, but the police would still be completely in the dark about the North, East, and South Sides, to say nothing of the narcotics, the fencing operation, or the links to mobs in other locales. Even high-level informers such as Joseph Valachi can only tell so much, and much of this information is not of the sort that can lead to a successful prosecution.

Arrests in one area do not affect another. In recent years there have been several million-dollar drug busts, in which the lawnmen have captured large quantities of drugs as well as arresting those transporting them. This has not led to a large-scale dismantling of the drug syndicates. The mobs just plug the hole and carry on. Compartmentalization is what keeps the various operations of the mob from going down like a row of dominoes.

c) Coercion. This is the main entorcement tool of organized crime, as it is of legitimate government. The word is out: "If you talk, you die." It is really rule by terror and the mob acts like a mini-government, or perhaps an occupation force would be a better likeness.

The rule of silence even extends to those who are not members of the mob. Unaffiliated witnesses are found to have mysteriously lost their memories, if the case comes to trial. Investigations often come to a halt much earlier because people who were there insist that they didn't see anything.

Sometimes this is because the witnesses have been directly threatened, but sometimes it is because of a vague fear on the part of the witness. He has heard about what happens to people who talk . . .

The most celebrated case is that of Arnold Shuster, a shoe-store clerk in Brooklyn who identified Willie Sutton, the bank robber, for the police several decades ago. Willie Sutton was arrested and one day Shuster was shot to death outside a subway station, probably in retaliation and as a warning to others.

The Federal government's response to this has been to set up the Witness Protection Program for important witnesses who fear for their lives. It is of very limited effectiveness because it is used only for the most important witnesses in the major cases. It has no effect on the small crimes.

As a sidelight to this, years ago when gangs plagued New York the police were sometimes able to use counter-intimidation to confront the gangsters who attempted to intimidate witnesses. At the time, for example, the West Side gangs ran a protection racket among the shopkeepers of certain sections of the city. The New York Police Department had a special unit set up to fight these gangs—the Broadway Squad. These were tough and capable detectives who became legends in their own time. One of them, "Broadway Johnny" Broderick, was reknown for dealing out "curbstone justice". When he had a case against a gangster who tried to frighten a witness he would confront the hood in an alley and give him a stern warning, reinforced with kicks and punches, that if he interfered with the witness he would spend the next six months in the hospital.

Forty or fifty years ago this worked: today it would be almost impossible, with the rise of concern for the rights of criminals. Any policeman who behaved in this manner would be open to both a civil suit and criminal prosecution. He would be disowned by his department and his career would be over.

d) Co-option. One important reason why organized crime is so hard to prosecute is that basically they are giving the people what they want. It is painless crime, in many cases. Some parts of it are even seen as legitimate by many people.

The modern era of organized crime in this country began with prohibition, when an ill-advised government banned a substance that most people would commit a crime to obtain. The moonshine traffic flourished because of the continued support of millions of satisfied customers. Prohibition was finally repealed, and not a moment too soon, but organized crime was on its way and soon found other fields of endeavor.

The mainstay of organized crime is vice. It is impossible to define where vice stops and where pleasure begins, or vice versa! Let's look at a short list of products and pleasures that have been touched by organized crime at one time or another and consider how many people would react to them:

Beer

Whiskey

Marijuana

Pornography

Cocaine

Used car parts

Heroin

"Pirate" tapes and recordings

Dexedrine

Stolen cars

Fencing "hot" goods of all types

Hijacking

It is easy to say that Hijacking is robbery, that Heroin is deadly and should be outlawed. Yet, there are many well-meaning people who say that Marijuana does no harm, that Alcohol in all its forms is a legitimate pastime, and that Pornography is not harmful, even for children. That is the main reason for the great success of organized crime. Pleasure blends slowly and imperceptibly into vice, and the syndicate covers the whole spectrum. They are experts at giving the people what they want and more importantly, will pay money to get.

The problem of differentiating pleasure from vice is an impossible one. A simple way is simply to draw the line at legality and say that whatever is legal is okay and what is illegal is wrong. Even that is not good enough, as laws vary from state to state. Gambling and prostitution are illegal in many states: they are both legal in Nevada. Alcohol is banned in some counties in our Southern states: it is legal everywhere else.

Whether it is legal or illegal, moral or immoral, there is money to be made and the mob is making it with our help. Each of us has his personal standard. There are some things we would not buy; some things we would not do. Yet there are things we would do and buy: we all love bargains and when one comes along we do not inquire too closely as to whether the merchandise is "hot". Some of us feel that a puff on a "joint" is all right for an adult to do, once in a while. Most of us know people who do use illegal drugs in one form or another. While we may not be surrounded by hard-core addicts, many people do use Mary Jane or something else with discretion. It is impossible to draw the line.

It is when the mob moves into the supporting functions that it is easy to see how the harm is done. The car that is broken up as a source of cheap spare parts at a "chop shop" has to have been stolen from somebody. If, during the process of illegally copying and reselling popular tapes, someone gets greedy and tries to pocket more than his share of the proceeds, he won't be fired: he'll be dropped into the river or buried in an unmarked grave out in the toolies. The porn "star" who balks at making another film may have acid thrown in her face, or be threatened with something worse. A participant in a drug buy who gets "burned" may kill the party trying to burn him. Someone involved in a jurisdictional dispute between two rival mobs winds up in the hospital or the morgue.

It is when we come to white-collar crime that it really gets sticky. To begin with, white-collar crime has always gotten less attention than violent crime. A shooting is much more spectacular and gets more attention in the press than an embezzlement or a case of price-fixing, even though the money involved in a white-collar crime is usually more. Also, people react less forcefully to having their money chiseled away from them penny by penny than at gunpoint, for perfectly understandable reasons.

Finally, most white-collar crime is covered by a different set of laws. Robbery, drug dealing, and hijacking are all felonies: so is embezzlement. Bribery of a company officer is harder to define, and harder yet to prove. Price-fixing is covered by another section of the law entirely. Industrial espionage, if prosecuted, will have to be covered under "trespassing" or a civil suit will have to be made. The biggest white-collar criminals are never arrested by tough-faced policemen who burst in on them with sirens screaming and guns drawn. They are never taken away in handcuffs. Instead, they may be summoned to an "administrative hearing" in the offices of some government agency such as the SEC or the FDA. Then if it goes against them, they may be asked to sign a consent decree, which is a legal form in which the accused does not admit guilt but promises not to do it again.

Most of the laws are aimed at protecting a business from its employees or the public, not the reverse. A simple example will illustrate this point:

A restaurant employee who takes food home with him without the permission of management can be arrested and taken away in handcuffs. If the management does not pay him on time, though, he cannot call the police. He has to report it to the labor board and hope that they can shake it up for him. Whether or not he still has a job next week is another matter. The same restaurant can call the police to arrest someone who leaves without paying the bill. If a customer complains that the restaurant listed butter on the menu but served him margarine, however, he can't call the cops. He might carry his complaint to the Better Business Bureau, or the State Attorney General's office, where action will be slow, very slow.

Another example will help to show the extent of the problem and how it affects us all:

Someone who takes a can of anchovies or a box of candy from a supermarket without paying for it will be arrested and jailed if he is caught. If the supermarket sells a customer a container of sour milk, the manager will not be taken away in handcuffs. The Board of Health may get involved and may send an inspector to check out the complaint . . .

Some police departments and some prosecutors' offices are starting to train their staffs in investigating and prosecuting the few white-collar crimes that are covered under existing laws, but it is a feeble effort compared to the size of the problem. Some private agencies just scratch at the surface, A white-collar criminal will not fear Ralph Nader as he would five years in the slammer.

The crime problem is serious and it is growing. Some claim that the number of crimes hasn't increased but only the number being reported, giving the impression that crime is growing. Even if that is correct, it is of little satisfaction. A crime rate that has stabilized at a high level is only slightly less frightening than one which is growing. To the person who has been victimized by a criminal, the statistics mean nothing and it will not make him feel any better to be told that the police are neither winning or losing the war on crime, but are merely marking time.

5. Capital Punishment

It is essential to take a fast look at capital punishment because so often that is the sentence that vigilantes hand out. Of course, approval or disapproval of capital punishment is a highly individual matter and opinion in this country is sharply divided on this issue.

Those who oppose capital punishment say that it is a practice unworthy of a civilized society, while those who favor it point to the alleged deterrent value.

Ironically enough, those who favor it strongly, which includes most policemen, do so out of a sense of compassion for the victim of the crime. It is being belatedly realized that much attention has been focused on the rights of the criminal and that meanwhile the victim has been forgotten. Capital punishment is an obvious deterrent and presumably will save other potential victims.

It will be a source of controversy for at least the next century whether we are truly civilized or merely organized. No doubt there are civilized people among us: no doubt it is difficult to place that label on many of the criminals who infest our society. It is particularly difficult to think of mass murderers as products of a civilized society. Still, it is possible to dismiss mass murderers as individual aberrations, people who are "sick in the head" and not typical of society as a whole. It is harder to ignore vast criminal conspiracies that commit murder and other crimes for profit. If they are sick, then we are all sick, and that is absurd.

It has been fashionable in recent years to label America as "a sick society" as an explanation for various aberrations. Apart from the fact that it is impossible to sum up a society of well over two hundred million people in one sentence, it is sloppy thinking to place everybody in the same category. A phrase such as: "Our society is stripping its gears" has a nice sound to it and is very convincing, despite the superficiality of its judgment.

It is when we look at the members of our society individually that this sort of sloppy logic breaks down. We see that not every person who came up from the slums is a member of Murder, Inc. and that not everyone with an Italian or Jewish surname is a member of organized crime. In fact, the hardcore criminals are a minority and a small one at that. They are the true non-conformists in what we like to think of as the greatest civilization that this planet has had.

The career criminal is at home with the technology of the Twentieth Century but his mentality is back in the jungle. Superficially, he looks like the rest of us but he is not one of us. As a practical matter, attempts at reforming him have failed and death is the only sure way to end his career.

This is not a very radical notion. Many states have laws to the effect that repeat offenders are liable to life imprisonment. The "three-time-losers" go to the slammer and society throws away the key. Many people consider prison a living death. It is hard to see how physical death can be much worse.

6. The "Criminal Justice System"

After the police comes the rest of the much criticized "criminal justice system". Theoretically, this is supposed to process the accused and determine his guilt or innocence by a trial, and if he is guilty to mete out the appropriate punishment. In practice many people are dissatisfied with the results. Some of the problems are due to built-in weaknesses and others result from saturation.

The first gap in performance is bail. Many offenders arrested for serious crimes are soon out on bail while their cases wait their turns on the court calendars. The police, in particular, are exasperated by this: "The guy's out on bail almost before I finish writing my report." It is easy to blame this failing on "soft-headed judges" but the fact is that there is not enough jail space to house all the offenders, so only the most serious ones can be kept in custody. Another, and more serious defect in the system is that it discriminates in favor of the affluent criminal, who has no trouble getting up the money to bail himself out.

Trials are pretty much a farce today. To begin with, the courts are crowded, and that means endless delays even under the best of circumstances in our nation's large cities. Moreover, the laws allow postponements of trials for a variety of reasons and excuses and this leads to further abuses, including delays of a year or more before the case comes to trial. The basic problem, though, is that it costs money to run a court, just as it does a jail or a prison, and the taxpayers are reluctant to pay more for a bigger system. Without additional money, the system will stay saturated and overcrowded.

The feature of the courts that has been the most criticized is the plea-bargaining system, in which the prosecution offers

23

the offender a "deal", whereby in return for pleading guilty and saving the state the expense of a trial the accused faces a lesser charge than the original one and a reduced sentence. This is not, as some people think, an informal and under-the-table affair. Plea-bargaining involves a sort of "price list", with the market fluctuating somewhat with the season and local conditions, and with a formal agreement being signed by the parties in some jurisdictions. Plea-bargaining would be unnecessary if the courts and prisons were not overflowing as they are now. It is an expedient measure for speeding up the traffic, and as some would say: "Necessity knows no law".

If the case comes to trial, it is not really tried on its merits in some cases, but on the situation of the offender. Some exasperated observers feel that justice is deaf, dumb, and blind, that her seeing eye dog is dead and that she left her white cane at home. The trial system does not guarantee justice for all, only better treatment for the affluent. The poor offender has to rely on the services of the Public Defender, a court-appointed lawyer who handles the case for a minimal fee. The Public Defender rarely gives it all he's got, but usually advises his client on the state of the current market in plea-bargaining, and he tries to work the best "deal" he can for his client. The affluent criminal, on the other hand, can afford to hire a high-priced lawyer who will do something to justify his lavish fee. Most of the time, the party who has the better lawyer wins the case.

The worst irony of this phase of the system is that the career criminal who is released on bail pending trial uses the time and opportunity to raise money to pay for his defense—by committing more crimes, of course.

Despite the supposition that every case will be tried on its merits and that the sentence will fit not only the crime but the criminal, there exist informal sentencing guidelines for judges to follow. These, unfortunately, are dictated by the conditions of overcrowding in the prisons rather than by other considerations.

The "graybar hotels" can house only so many people and they are filled to capacity most of the time. In some cases, inmates are shoehorned in and the prisons are overcrowded, leading to some recent Federal Court rulings that the inmate population be reduced by any means possible. This usually has meant early release.

Leading to the overcrowding are two factors: one major and one minor. The first is that there are simply too many people being sentenced by the courts for the existing facilities. The prisons were built to handle the caseload of the nineteen-forties. The main reason that there are not enough prison beds is financial. It costs more to keep a man in prison than in college. The taxpayers, already overburdened, rebel at paying even more into the prison system.

The other reason accounts for a small but ever-increasing proportion of the prison population; those who are there for life but who otherwise would have been executed. The decade-long moratorium on capital punishment in this country, and the limited, lukewarm resumption of executions have added their quota to the prison population. Many who would have occupied a cell for only a few weeks and then left the prison feet first, are now in there for life.

So we have people who would normally be sentenced to a prison term being given probation because prison capacity is reserved only for the most serious offenders, and at the other end of the line felons are being released from prison by parole boards under pressure to generate more space by emptying out the prisons of all but the most hopeless cases.

The parole boards come in for a share of flak every time a parolee committs a particularly heinous or noteworthy crime. They are accused of being "liberal", "soft-headed", and various other names that are also applied to their colleagues on the bench who cannot impose stiffer sentences.

"Time off for good behavior" is another way that inmates serve less than their sentences, but it is built into the system as a means of control. The inmate has an incentive to behave himself in order to gain early release. In itself, this is a good thing and is much desired by prison administrators.

The bottom line, however, is that of all the serious crimes reported, only about a quarter are cleared by arrest and only a small proportion of the arrestees wind up serving time. The numbers vary from year to year but the number who see the inside of a prison hovers around one or two percent.

The criminal justice system is saturated: stiffer laws are of no use in the long run, as we can't adequately enforce the ones we have.

Apologists for the system, such as Charles F. Silberman, author of "Criminal Violence, Criminal Justice", Random House, 1978, like to say that the criminal gets caught in the end and that proves the system works. They claim that the police can make many mistakes but the criminal needs to make only one, and he gets caught.

Unfortunately, while the police are making their mistakes, people are getting hurt, either physically or economically. Their property is being ripped off and if they are unfortunate, so are their lives and health.

The choices open to the people are all unpleasant. More cops, courts, and prisons mean more taxes. Execution of career criminals is a program that is not likely to be adopted in a society that has been programmed to care more for the rights of the criminal than those of his victim.

Historically, when the machinery for enforcing the law has broken down or has proved to be inadequate, the people have taken up the task of enforcing the law themselves. That is the subject of the next chapter.

7. "As American As Apple Pie"

Vigilantes have existed in America since the early days, which is only to be expected in a developing country with a lawless frontier and some of whose citizens were the outcasts from other nations.

The British used to deport some of their criminals to the colonies: we got our share. Others came to this country fleeing from justice in their native lands.

Vigilantes were not always called that: the older name was "regulators", and it was first applied before the Revolutionary War. One of the instances in which the regulators enforced the law was in South Carolina around 1867. Criminal justice was a pretty primitive thing in those days, depending upon a sheriff and a local magistrate, or justice of the peace. Even these were unavailable in the South Carolina back country, so a regulator movement arose to do the job that the government was unable to do. It seemed quite normal and natural to have regulators in those days because government was still thought of as deriving its power from the people and the people were, in the most direct sense, the upholders of the government, the militia, and the law enforcement authority, unlike today.

An obscure character named Lynch, again of the Revolutionary War era, had his name borrowed to denote the practice of summary execution, Lynching. Lynching has an ugly sound, and the word is usually used to denote a killing of which one disapproves. If the man's name had been "Fair" or "Justice", or "Judge", all good old Anglo-Saxon names, would stringing-up have such a bad name today?

In regard to lynching, it is a myth that all vigilantes summarily hanged their subjects, or suspects, as the case may

27

be. A "quotation", probably spurious, that is used to support this view is: "First we'll give 'em a fair trial and then we'll hang 'em." Nobody seems to know who originally said this or when.

Actually, there have been times when after a trial by vigilantes the defendant was found innocent and released. One such was in San Francisco on February 23, 1851. Two men, Windred and Stuart, accused of robbing and murdering a shopkeeper, were tried by a vigilante jury and acquited.

San Francisco of the 1850's was not the lawless frontier, however, and the San Francisco Committee of Vigilance was probably the first instance of Vigilantism in the modern style. It came into being because, although San Francisco had a municipal government with courts and a police department, the police were ineffective in fighting crime. The town's leading citizens, including the mayor himself, endorsed and even participated in enforcing the law when the police did not.

Montana in 1863 might have still been considered the frontier but the fact is that the various jurisdictions had their local governments and law enforcement officers. The trouble with Virginia City, however, was that the sheriff, Henry Plummer, was actually the leader of the band of thieves and murderers that plagued the area that year. The situation got so bad that by the end of the year some of the citizens got together in secret and formed a committee to enforce the law that the Sheriff was flouting. They were a very brave little band because the criminal gang was so large that the vigilantes were outnumbered about three to one. This disproves another myth about vigilantes; that they invariably were a howling mob descending upon one or two hapless victims and overwhelming them by sheer numbers. Sometimes they did. Sometimes also, as in this example, they were like guerrillas fighting against a criminal army of occupation.

After some sharp skirmishes the crooked sheriff got his, being hanged on January 10, 1864. Unfortunately, the vigilantes got carried away after a while and started hanging people for minor offenses, the sort of thing which gives vigilantism a bad name. In the balance, though, Montana was

28

better off with the vigilantes than it had been with Henry Plummer, who in abusing his office contributed to the deaths of many innocent men.

Another feature of the Montana vigilante operations that has been criticized is the scouring of the surrounding area for the members of the Plummer Gang, with some vigilantes going as far as Denver. Granted that it was not absolutely necessary to pursue the criminals such a long distance to rid the territory of them, it does reflect upon the mentality of the people of those days. Chasing the hoodlums out of town and into someone else's territory was just dumping the problem upon their neighbors' laps. The vigilantes had more of a sense of responsibility than that, and saw to it that their problem did not become someone else's problem.

The events in New Orleans in 1890 have been given the "vigilante" label but perhaps they don't deserve it. A mob invaded the jail in which suspects in the slaying of a well-liked police official were being held. The mob shot or hanged eleven men that day, and it is obvious that some of those killed were innocent. Unfortunately, it is very easy to apply a label to someone and the label tends to stick, which does not make getting an undistorted view of the facts any easier.

One might think that with the coming of the Twentieth Century vigilantism would become obsolete. The frontier was closing and law enforcement officials were everywhere in the land, making do-it-yourself justice unnecessary. It has turned out not to be so. Now, more than ever, the need and opportunity for do-it-yourself justice is there, as the problems of the frontier give way to the problems of urban crime, organized crime, and white-collar crime. The police, for their increase in numbers and, incidentally, operating budgets, seem less able to control crime than their earlier counterparts.

The population of the country has increased in the Twentieth Century: so has the number of criminals and the number of vigilantes. Vigilantes are operating on the streets of America today and that is what we shall examine closely in Part Two.

PART II.
VIGILANTISM TODAY

Introduction

This section is about what is going on today. It deals not with what should be but what is. It tells what citizens are doing to defend themselves against crime, and what they are doing in the cases where they counterattack.

Counterattack is the central idea behind the practice of vigilantism. It is easy to say that we will only act to defend ourselves if directly threatened. The fact is that the criminal who threatens our neighbor will threaten us tomorrow.

It has been said that vigilantism is the response of frightened men, as if to belittle the vigilante and all he stands for. Actually, anyone who is not frightened by crime is simply not aware of how serious the problem is, or has not had it hit him directly. The person who has been mugged, or the householder who has come home to find his residence broken into and his possessions gone, is frightened. The city dweller who puts three or four locks on his door and is cautioned never to open the door without knowing who is on the other side is certainly frightened. This is a legitimate fear.

In real life, unlike in the movies, we are not all John Waynes or Gary Coopers ready to punch or shoot it out with the bad guys. We are not all muscular he-men who can engage in protracted physical combat with a gang of hoodlums and come out on top. We may be assaulted in a dark hallway at ten o'clock at night. For us High Noon may come in a crowded subway station during the five o'clock rush.

Typically, criminals attack from a position of strength. They either outnumber the victim or take him or her by surprise.

The criminal often operates by stealth, waiting and choosing his moment with care. He will not attack when the

33

police are around and he will not attack when the intended victim is expecting him.

When the organizations that the citizens pay to defend them against crime fail to do so; when the police are seen to be unable to even defend themselves, then some of the more concerned citizens will undertake to enforce the law themselves.

Many efforts have been made to discredit the citizen who enforces the law himself. He has been maligned by the police, who do not like it revealed that they are not doing an adequate job. He is criticized by lawyers and jurists whose livelihood directly depends upon the criminal justice system as it exists right now. He gets flak from psychologists and social workers who earn their keep by trying to rehabilitate the criminal, while treating the victim of a crime with a majestic unconcern.

The justification for vigilantism will not be found in the Bible, the Constitution, or even in Common Law. There has been some published material about the "posse comitatus" being rooted in Common Law, but that does not apply today. Common Law had its origin in medieval times and is of only historical interest today.

Actually, the Constitution and Common Law can be interpreted (a better word would be twisted) to mean anything at all, to support any point of view. Lawyers are very good at doing this. A lawyer will find an interpretation of the law to suit the needs of the party who is paying his fee.

The primary law of human behavior is that people do what they want to do and find justification for it afterwards.

In reality, the only justification for vigilantism is a practical one; the urgent need for action. For those who like slogans, there is; "Necessity knows no law." What this means in practical terms here and now is not a matter of 'necessity inducing people into taking reckless and immoral measures, but prudent reaction to correct a bad situation, in which the traditional criminal justice system no longer functions adequately.

This section is about what real people are doing about real crime today. It is based on fact. Part of it is based on the author's experience in vigilante actions. It is important, when writing a book on a controversial subject such as this, for the author to maintain a low profile and not to write what would be a detailed confession. Therefore, some of the incidents described will not be described accurately as regards location or exact time of occurrence, and some names will be either changed or omitted to protect living people who did their best to cope with a bad situation.

The author has known some people who took part in some vigilante actions, both with him and with other groups. They are very ordinary seeming people who could easily be anyone's neighbor and who lead very ordinary lives, but who, like the author, have found themselves in situations in which they felt obliged to arm themselves and to be mentally and physically prepared to shoot it out with the criminal.

8. What Vigilantes Are Not

In Part One we laid the groundwork for a definition of what today's vigilante is. Here we will narrow it down a bit further by specifying what a vigilante is not, dispelling some of the mythology that has arisen on the subject.

Vigilantes are not citizens who "take the law into their own hands". They do not make up the law. They enforce the law as it exists when the law enforcement agencies are ineffective.

Vigilantes are not politicians who abuse the powers of their offices to persecute those who do not agree with them.

Vigilantes are not night riders who persecute people because of their ethnic or religious affiliations.

Vigilantes are not members of lynch mobs or participants in any kind of public disorder.

It is necessary to specify what vigilantes are not because the term has been applied so loosely to any sort of group violence by those who do not know better. The result has been that instead of vigilantes being seen as an honorable part of our history they have been lumped together with the very people they were combatting.

We will take a look at the vigilante in fiction to see how he looks in fantasy. We will look at the vigilante as he actually exists today.

9. What Vigilantes Are

A good working definition of vigilantes in one sentence is: "Citizens who commit felonies to enforce the law in the absence or failure of the formal mechanism of law enforcement." This is the best that can be done in one sentence and it requires some explanation. It also leaves some loose ends, as there are always gray areas in the law and the situations of those who break it.

Vigilantes commit acts that would be considered felonies, just as the police do. Killing someone is a felony. Using force to take him from one place to another is a felony. Police do these things, and more, but by virtue of their office they are exempt from the law. When a policeman or a prosecutor makes a "deal" with a suspect, offering him immunity or a reduced charge in return for information about other criminals, that is extortion, but because of the way it is done, who is doing it, and the reason for doing it, it is not considered to be illegal. Vigilantes do not have the protection of the law as an umbrella for their actions. Under the law they are fully liable for their acts. In practice they are rarely prosecuted because it is the failure of the mechanism of the law that prompted the vigilantes to act in the first place.

Citizens who become vigilantes do not make up the law or, as so often charged, "take the law into their own hands." That implies that they take the law for their own selfish purposes. Actually, they are enforcing the law by other means.

Vigilantes arise in a power vacuum. When the conventional machinery of law and order breaks down or does not exist, that does not erase the need to enforce the laws and deal with lawbreakers, at least the serious ones. This is a point worth repeating because it is the central idea behind vigilantes. Vigilantes are not hooligans or blood thristy killers. They are more or less ordinary citizens who see the need to enforce the law and feel that if they don't do it, it won't get done.

We have seen how there was a need for direct action on the frontier. We see today that in some cities there are corrupt or ineffective police departments and that this leads to the citizens doing their own policing. We can, by comparing different cities in our country, see that some police departments are much more or much less effective than others in combatting crime.

We must recognize, too, that there are organizations that operate on the fringe of vigilantism. "Operation Blockwatch" and similar programs, conducted with the guidance and blessing of the police, are examples of citizens involved in do-it-yourself law enforcement. What differentiates them from the pure vigilantes is that the vigilantes are police, judge, jury and executioner all in one. That is the dividing line. Quasi-vigilantes are content to turn their catches over to the police, or to summon the police for help. They are still working within the system and the system can still cope with the situation, with this minimal help from the citizenry.

10. Today's Vigilantes In Fiction

It might seem strange to find a long chapter on fiction in a book devoted to fact, but there is a good reason for this. The fiction that people read is one guide to their mood. It gives a good idea of what they're thinking and, even to what some of them will do in the near future. Recent events bear this out.

On the most basic level comic-strip heroes are vigilantes. Superman, Batman, and the like are glorious, uniformed figures who, although they do not have any official capacity, enforce the law when the police run into a particularly difficult problem or a particularly vicious criminal. They mete out instant justice, too, giving the evildoers a quick beating before hustling them off to the lockup. Of course, in the comic strip, the police and the public are properly grateful to these crusaders, unlike in real life.

Most people outgrow these super heroes pretty quickly but the theme of summary justice outside the formal structure of the law persists. From the earliest decades of this century, the exploits of "private eyes" who grapple with criminals and solve cases when the police are baffled has been a staple of popular literature. These fictional private investigators are much more altruistic than their real-life counterparts and much more willing to risk life and limb for the sake of truth and justice. They sometimes are portrayed as a thorn in the side of the police because they are so effective when the cops are not, and they often use unconventional methods denied to the official police.

One outstandingly successful character of the past three decades has been Mike Hammer, the creation of the well-known Mickey Spillane. He has an uneasy relationship with the police, despite a personal friendship with the head of the homicide squad, because of his brutal and bloody methods of furthering an investigation. Inevitably he leaves a trail of bodies behind him but fortunately they are all bad guys who deserve what they get at the hands of Mike Hammer. These novels have sold tens of millions of copies, showing that people are interested in a private approach to the crime problem.

Mike Hammer, although somewhat outlandish in his methods, is not a pure fantasy hero. He has no super-powers such as the ability to leap a tall building, etc. He is of the hard-boiled realism school of fictional characters. All in all, he is less unrealistic than some of the later developments.

In recent years there have been a number of novels by "Mainstream" writers dealing with vigilante actions by people who have been hurt in some way be criminals. Most of the time they deal with a solid, middle-class citizen who suffers a personal loss from vicious street crime and undertakes to get revenge. One such is "The Shrewsdale Exit", by John Buell, (Pocket Books), in which a man's wife and daughter are killed by a gang of bikers. The bereaved father sets out to avenge their deaths and he succeeds in doing so.

The vengeance theme is carried a step further in another recent book, appropriately titled "With A Vengeance", by Gerald DiPego (Dell Books). A teen-age boy is brutally murdered by four other boys in a practical joke that turns into a vicious prank. The father bides his time and waits twenty years for revenge, until his son's killers are grown men and have families of their own.

The theme of a group of war buddies getting together to fight crime is expressed in several novels of recent years. One such is "The New Vigilantes" by James Horan, (Crown Publishers). A small clique of Vietnam veterans come back to the United States and are appalled at the vast changes that have taken place in the country while they were overseas. One of them is a millionaire, which helps a lot because the heroes do not have to worry about everyday pursuits such as jobs interfering with their vigilante activities. They decide to carry out a private war against a giant drug syndicate, culminating in a commando-style raid against the gang's cutting mill, which is located in a fortress-like building in New Jersey. In this novel, one note of realism is that the police do not turn a blind eye to their activities and the members of the group realize that they will be liable to prosecution if they are arrested.

Another story incorporating the "veterans" theme is "Sledgehammer", by Walter Wager (Pocket Books), in which a small group of ex-commandoes set out to avenge the death of one of their number, who has been slain by a criminal syndicate that is in control of a small town in the Deep South.

Some stories deal with vigilante actions by the police. It is logical enough that if private citizens see a need to short-circuit the formal mechanism of the law, that there should also be members of the official police who agree. One example of this type is; "Contract on Cherry Street", by Philip Rosenberg (Avon) in which a New York police inspector commanding an elite squad decides to take a few short-cuts in enforcing the law after a couple of decades of frustration in working within the system. He is in an advantageous position to do so, as he can use the machinery of the police department to help in his task and, being in a high executive position, can cover his tracks. His foe, as might be expected, is a criminal syndicate involved in disposing of hijacked merchandise. They have bought themselves virtual immunity from the machinery of the law as formally constituted but when the enterprising inspector takes up their case he is able to administer curbstone justice with no undue delay.

Another book of this genre is "Death Squad" by Herbert Kastle, in which a squad of policemen strike out on their own to bring justice to the bad guys.

In films, a similar theme is found in "Magnum Force", starring the ubiquitous Clint Eastwood of "Dirty Harry" fame. A quartet of patrolmen set out to eliminate the city's crime elite by gunning them down. In the story they find themselves at odds with Dirty Harry, whom they consider to be soft on crime. Harry fails to convince them of the error of their ways and the story ends in a big shoot-out in which Harry survives, of course, after eliminating the renegade cops. This story shows a certain unease with the vigilante theme, reflecting the feeling that although the end is admirable the methods used are not legitimate and that the formal mechanism of law and order, with all its faults, is the only way to go.

No such inhibitions mar the most successful series of Vigilante books of all time, the ones put out by Pinnacle Books. The story of the "Executioner", by Don Pendleton, sets the pattern for the rest. In this series, the first to come out of this publishing house, the hero, Mack Bolan, is a Vietnam veteran whose family has suffered because of the Mafia. He vows to fight a holy war against them until he is killed. His methods are simple and direct: death by shooting, bombing, artillery and rocket fire, and other assorted means suitable to the occasion. He raids the centers of Mafia activity, killing off the gang bosses as he finds them, and occasionally taking some of their money to finance his operations. He somehow has gotten an arsenal of weaponry that the rest of us can only envy. It is hard to see where one could get such an array of weapons without leaving some sort of a trace. He also drives a formidable vehicle known as his "war wagon", which has radar, rockets, and an armory that serves for all his needs. It is also, incidentally, a means of transportation and a place to eat and sleep.

Mack Bolan himself is a formidable man, over six feet tall, well-built, a former jungle fighter and Army sniper. He is wounded from time to time, but he always recovers and comes out on top. He acknowledges that his job will never end, that it will take him the better part of forever to wipe out the Mafia, but so far he has crusaded through over forty books in his never-ending war on organized crime.

There is in this country an "Executioner" cult, people who buy every volume in the series as soon as it comes out and who eagerly await the next one. This is a stunning success and it has prompted Pinnacle books to bring out a host of similar series.

Some of the others are:
"The Destroyer", by Sapir & Murphy
"The Vigilante", by V.J. Santiago
"The Butcher", by Stuart Jason
"The Death Merchant", by Rosenberger

Taken together these volumes have sold tens of millions of copies and, by the time this book appears in print the total may have passed one hundred million.

They all follow the same pattern—a more or less realistic hero, realistic in the sense that he does not wear a cape, outlandish uniform, have X-ray vision, etc., who carries on an unrelenting private war against an overwhelmingly powerful crime syndicate. The members of the syndicate are presented as unquestionably evil people, the sort who torture women, kill children, and tear the wings off flies. Many of them have ethnic names, such as Amorosi, Benelli, and even Santoro. Our heroes are provided with the most modern weaponry and they know how to use them. They do not have to work for a living, having their own private means, and even taking subsistence from the enemy. In most cases they are hunted by the police, who are as ineffective in tracking them down as they are at coping with crime. There are a couple of sympathetic law enforcement officials, however, who give them clandestine help.

None of these "Executioner"-type heroes, however, has been as credible as Paul Benjamin, the central figure of Brian Garfield's classical "Death Wish". Paul Benjamin is not a superhero: he is, if anything, an anti-hero. He is an average, middleclass man in his forties, with no skill in martial arts to his credit and no experience with guns since his army service, many years ago. His wife is murdered by a gang of hoodlums and his only daughter is driven insane by the trauma of the incident. Paul is in profound grief and barely able to cope with the situation. He does not understand why this has happened to him and his family. Before this, he had been insulated from the effects of violent crime and he had not given it much thought. Now he decides that he will do something about it.

On a business trip to Arizona, he meets a man who tells him a bit of the frontier spirit and shows him how to shoot a pistol. When he goes back to New York the man gives him the pistol and some ammunition to take with him. Back in Fun City, Paul takes to the streets in search of muggers and street hoodlums of the sort who murdered his wife. He realizes that his chances of finding the very ones who killed her are small, and that he cannot rid the city of crime by himself, but he makes a start. He does not have any super-weapon, super-skill, or semi-magical source of finance. He still goes to work and prowls the parks and alleys after dark seeking out the predators. Sometimes he catches some of them in the act of preying on another: sometimes he acts as a decoy to attract them, shooting them when they try to mug him. Having the advantage of surprise, he is very successful in his campaign. He kills a number of them before the police start to react. As one might expect in real life, their response is one of disapproval. They are, of course, embarrassed at the fact of a private citizen doing their job for them and in particular, doing it so well. Add to this the fact that what Paul is doing is a felony and you have a situation in which although Paul's actions are approved by and reassuring to many citizens, and even some policemen, Paul himself is in a legally indefensible position.

What makes this book and its sequel "Death Sentence", so notable is that it is so realistic. The story tells in minute detail how one man, who has to work for a living as do the rest of us, goes about eliminating street hooligans. He does not have any super-powers or any advantages over the rest of us. He is over forty and physically past his prime: he is non-descript, a man who would blend in with a hundred others in a subway car, and yet he takes effective and decisive action in a way that is understandable to everyone.

The book was so successful that it was made into a movie. The film followed the plot and the details of the book quite well, with only a few changes, one of which was to change the hero's surname from Benjamin to Kersey, which is not Jewish, perhaps in an attempt to give the film more popular appeal. In any event the film added to Charles Bronson's reputation and has been replayed on television many times.

"Death Wish" can serve as a how-to manual for urban vigilantes. None of the scenes described are impossible or implausible. It is all very realistic. Perhaps it has led to some real-life imitators.

11. Today's Vigilantes In Fact -
A Few Vignettes

The Guardian Angels—Few would deny that New York City is one of the most awful places to live in the civilized world. Today street crime is so bad that the police have been going in pairs for decades. Someplaces in the city are just too dangerous to penetrate after dark. The subway system is one such place. A group calling itself "The Guardian Angels", and wearing white T-shirts and red berets has taken on the task of trying to make the subways a bit safer by patrolling them. They are unarmed and unloved by the police and by City Hall. Mayor Koch has spoken disapprovingly of them and they get no cooperation and much harassment from the police. They have had some successes against violent crime in the subways but no acknowledgement of their effectiveness by City Hall.

Phoenix, Arizona is a pleasant place to live, in many ways. Its rate of violent crime is very low. However, its rate of non-violent crime has, in some recent years, been the highest in the nation. Petty theft and vandalism are common. In one section of north-west Phoenix recently a group of neighbors banded together to do something about it themselves, as the police apparently were not able to patrol the area intensively enought to prevent much of the vandalism. The affair was featured on the television news, the participants were labelled vigilantes, and so far the results seem to be inconclusive.

Some parts of the Bronx, New York, are the worst in the city. The south-west corner of the Bronx is the location of the real-life "Fort Apache" made notorious in the film of the same name. In 1974, three men were arrested for administering beatings to drug addicts and pushers in that area. They called themselves "vigilantes".

In New York City, there have been many cases of addicts and pushers killed without the perpetrators being identified or arrested. There is no way to tell how many of these were a result of vigilante action.

In the Crown Heights section of Brooklyn the residents, who are mostly ultra-orthodox Jews, became so alarmed by the increase in street crime in their area that they established their own neighborhood street patrols, calling themselves the Maccabees. They equipped themselves with cars and radios and even a command post, and went about trying to make the streets of their neighborhood safe for women and children. Predictably, the police expressed their disapproval, even though it was their failure that prompted the formation of this group in the first place. After a year of effort, the concensus was that the patrols had been effective in reducing crime in the area. They had made several arrests and turned the criminals over to the police and the streets were somewhat safer for the effort.

An extensive listing of present-day vigilantes who have appeared in the news media will be found in chapter ten of William Burrows' book, "Vigilante". Unfortunately, the ones that make the news are not necessarily the most effective ones. Vigilantes shun publicity and the ones which are publicized are often not true vigilantes. An "Operation Blockwatch", sponsored by the police, is not a vigilante operation by our definition, as the participants do not enforce the law themselves but merely call the police when they see a crime being committed. Yet, they may get a lot of officially sponsored publicity. On the other hand, a criminal who is quietly eliminated, with the body buried in an isolated spot fifty miles from nowhere will not be featured in the news at all, unless he is a well-known figure whose "disappearance" arouses some curiosity.

The lessons that are to be learned from the publicly acknowledged instances of "vigilante" action can be reduced to a few sentences:

1) Publicity does not help.

2) Publicity can be harmful.

3) Members of a vigilante group who become publicly identified will lose their effectiveness.

4) The police will usually not help.

5) The police and other public officials will hinder, if anything, and will prosecute the vigilante if they can.

6) The most effective vigilantes are the ones about which you never hear.

Note: As this book went to press, a news story appeared to the effect that the New York City police are going to train the "Guardian Angels" mentioned earlier and issue them some form of identification cards.

City hall officials, including the mayor, police commissioner, and the chief of the Transit Authority Police admitted that the Angels have done some good, have stopped over a hundred crimes or attempted crimes, and have been an effective deterrent to subway crime.

The Angels will still not be armed but are allegedly skilled in the martial arts. This is a step forward for the citizens who want to take direct action to protect themselves.

12. How Vigilante Groups Start

Vigilantes are not like other organizations. They usually do not have membership cards, badges, whistles and secret decoder rings. They do not have dues, as a rule. They do not advertise. An occasional exception can be found, as in the San Francisco Vigilantes of the last century, but usually vigilantes are clandestine organizations that shun publicity, and operate best out of the light of day.

Usually, a group of people see a threat from crime. The threat is usually severe and prolonged. The conventional machinery of the law does not do anything effective about the threat, for one reason or another. The people who will form the vigilante group get together, very informally, to discuss the situation. They are usually friends or neighbors. They do not call a formal meeting to organize a posse. Usually the process starts with a short discussion between two or three future members. They tentatively decide to act and set out to recruit others. Further meetings are held, a course of action is chosen, and then they act.

One example from not too many years ago occurred in a shop that was experiencing an epidemic of sabotage. Someone unknown was damaging the equipment. A group of employees who were close friends and who knew each other well enough to be sure that the saboteur was not one of them, decided to do something about it. As the continuing incidents of sabotage were causing suspicion to fall on all of them, this group decided, without the employer's knowledge, to stake out the shop after closing time in the hope of catching the saboteur in the act.

They brought pistols to work with them and, after closing time, concealed themselves on the premises, prepared to stay all night if need be. The logistics of the plan were simple — some sandwiches and thermos bottles of coffee, an extra clip of ammunition, and a lot of patience.

They staked out the shop for weeks. At first they hid inside. Later, they suspected that the perpetrator might have some way of telling that the building was still occupied, so they made a big show of leaving at the appointed hour and returned to stake out the shop from a parking lot across the avenue, selecting a vantage point between the other cars from which they could see all entrances to the shop.

There were a number of false alarms, in which it seemed that someone walking in the shadows of the building had forced an entry. When that happened, the vigilantes went roaring up to the building in their cars, the headlights covering all the exits, and proceeded to search the premises. There were some humorous incidents, such as the one in which the advance man of the search party climbed into a loft to search it only to discover that he was searching with any empty pistol in his hand. Before dismissing the group as a bunch of buffoons it must be noted that the two behind the lead man held pistols that were fully loaded, and for that reason any intruder discovered would have had to surrender immediately or be shot dead. The author was one of the search party, but happily, not the lead man.

The sabotage continued, despite the stakeouts, and the members of the group were forced to conclude that it was being done by someone who had legitimate access to the shop during business hours. The saboteur was never caught.

Another incident occurred during an epidemic of broken windshields. Someone was breaking auto windshields at night, usually on a Friday night, and the owners of cars in the block were concerned.

Several of them got together one day and decided to stake out the street the coming Friday night. The stakeout followed the usual pattern. The members of the group selected vantage points from which they could see the whole street, parked their cars so that they could either cut off escape or pursue anyone they caught smashing a windshield. They equipped themselves with clubs, a rifle, sandwiches and

13. Do-It-Yoursef Justice

Many people have reservations about being self-appointed police, judges, juries, and executioners. Out of an admirable but possibly misguided sense of fair play, they may feel that they are denying the criminal a "Fair Trial", with a chance to defend himself and all the other privileges that go with being the defendant in an American trial.

It is critically important to distinguish between law and order and the symbols of law and order, true justice and the symbols of justice. A person who has committed a crime is not any more guilty because he has been officially declared guilty by a judge and jury who were not there when the crime was committed. On the contrary, there are many opportunities for slips and errors in the formal mechanism of justice.

When a crime is committed and the criminal gets away for the moment, and the victim gives a description to the police, an arrest may follow in a few days on the basis of that description. Then the victim is confronted with the suspect, who may resemble the criminal. The victim may identify him as such, but many cases of mistaken identity have in fact occurred in exactly this way. A vigilante who applies rough-and-ready justice to a perpetrator whom he catches in the act is not denying the criminal justice in any sense of the word. A fair trial in this case would merely be a redundancy, an unnecessary complication.

Some will complain that the punishment applied by vigilantes is too severe and they may be right. It is also true that many feel that the punishment applied by the courts is too lenient. It is a fact that many crimes go totally unpunished because the criminal never sees the inside of a courtroom.

The question of severity of punishment is one that must be decided by the vigilante in the individual case. It is probable that it will be fair, because vigilantes are not blood-thirsty maniacs as some would claim, but ordinary people just like us, who are exasperated at the slow and hesitant process of formal justice.

There have been many complaints about police brutality, and the brutality built into the existing criminal justice system. Some of these complaints are valid. There have been arrestees who have received far more than most people would feel they deserved for their crime at the hands of brutal police and sadistic prison guards. From this perspective, vigilante justice is not as harsh and inhuman as some would believe.

14. Who Are Today's Vigilantes?

The theory has come about that vigilantes are the elite of society practicing repression upon the poor, the nonconformists, the outcasts, and the disenfranchised. This may have been true to some extent at one time, and if you look at the history of the frontier it is easy to see how such a judgment might be formed.

The classical vigilante was the community's leading citizen defending himself and his property against criminals. The banker, rancher, shopkeeper, lawyer, formed vigilante posses to fight the criminal gangs that roamed the frontier in that area. The cowpunchers, the drifters, did not have a stake in preserving the community and so they often did not participate. It was not their fight.

The petty merchant and the rancher, primitive as they were, constituted the "establishment" of the frontier towns. By the standards of those days they were the elite.

"Elite" in this country has always meant economic elite—the most affluent members of society, never the most intelligent, the most practical, the most courageous, or the most honest. As we do not recognize royalty or a titled aristocracy, the dividing line between the elite and the common people is an economic one.

Today's economic elite don't practice vigilantism. They don't need to. Street crime is something that plagues the less affluent neighborhoods. You will never see a Rockefeller or a Mellon prowling the subway with a pistol in his pocket, waiting for a mugger to strike.

The rich neighborhoods are the best policed. Their country estates have electronic fences and private security guards. They own the government and the government works hard at protecting them. By contrast, the less affluent neighborhoods get what's left over in police and fire protection, and the residents are often left to cope as best they can with their problems. At election time the politicians come around to show their faces and to make the usual empty promises, and the rest of the time the lower class neighborhoods receive varying degrees of neglect from the government, except for the tax collection authorities.

Today's vigilante is not likely to be a member of the economic elite—more likely he is a member of the working or lower-middle class.

He is not likely to be the best "educated", either. "Education" in this country has come to be not only the process of teaching facts but certain attitudes too—a programming to inaction and conformity. "Education" has in part led to many people assuming a passive dependence upon the government and an expectation that they should not do anything for themselves; indeed, that it is wrong to do so. "Education" has led to a certain reversal of values, a belief that all the power and rights belong to the government and that the people only get what's left over.

Today's vigilante is likely to be a practical minded working man, a long time resident of his neighborhood who cares about what is happening around him. He is quite likely to have only a modest amount of formal education, but that does not mean that he is stupid. He may be very intelligent and self-educated, but not programmed. He is most likely to be a resident of a large city, for that is where the problems are the most acute. Today's frontier is on the asphalt, not on the prairie.

15. Selecting Targets

Today's vigilante usually does not have an agonizing choice in selecting his target or targets. The need dictates the choice. If his neighborhood is overrun with drug pushers he will not seek out a dishonest used-car dealer in the next county.

The most obvious type of target is the street criminal because his crime is usually against life as well as property and most people consider life more important than property. The check forger is usually seen as less of a threat than is the armed robber or the rapist.

Street criminals, for all the notoriety they get, are not as easy to find or to deal with as one might think. Vigilantes who take off after street crime are usually limited to standing or roving patrols, stakeouts, or decoy operations a la "Death Wish".

White-collar criminals are both easy to find and very vulnerable. They are easy targets and there is very little personal risk for the vigilante in dealing with the white-collar criminal.

The organized criminal is the hardest to destroy. He is not an individual but part of a large organization, insulated from and almost invulnerable to assault. Although attacks on organized crime leaders are the subject matter of much of the current fiction of vigilantism, in real life it hardly ever happens. One recent example was the bombing of the residence of Joseph Bonnano in Tucson by an FBI Agent striking off on his own.

A vigilante group striking at organized crime faces extraordinary difficulties because of several factors:

"Mr. Big" is well-protected. Sometimes his identity is not commonly known. He is hard to locate and usually has bodyguards.

Often the police will conduct an energetic search for the vigilantes, as they are in the pay of the syndicate.

The possibility of savage reprisals comes up if the identities of the vigilantes becomes known.

Still, with patience, security, and the proper tactics it is possible to strike at organized crime effectively. It has been done at various times and in various places. Vigilantes find that the best way to start is to strike at a satellite operation and then work in.

16. "Legitimate" Business

A certain legend has grown up about gangsters who "retire" and establish "legitimate" businesses, intending to "go straight". This myth has been spread by fiction writers and their readers, who enjoy the romantic notion that a hardened criminal, after a lifetime of preying on society, has an attack of conscience and sees the error of his ways. According to the legend, the gangster gathers up the profits of a criminal career, dissolves his associations with the mob, and invests in a legitimate business, becoming a "respected member of the community".

It is perfectly true that criminals do buy into businesses and that they often announce a retirement but this is usually a cover for something more sinister. An above-board company serves several purposes for the criminal:

a) An ostensible source of legitimate income to satisfy the tax authorities. A trafficker in illegal drugs cannot really put that down as an occupation on his income tax return, and if he does not file one he will find himself in serious trouble with the Federal Government, as Al Capone found out.

b) As a "front" for an illegal activity. A chain of appliance stores makes a good outlet for disposing of hijacked merchandise. A car dealership, with a thriving used car business on the side, can handle the output of a stolen-car ring. A body shop can cut up stolen cars for parts. A trucking company can furnish logistical support for a criminal activity, such as transportation for stolen merchandise.

c) A means of "laundering" illegally gotten money. Businesses that deal in cash, such as restaurants and many retail stores can, with a little creative accounting, show money funneled in from drug dealing, for example, as coming from the retail trade. Businesses dealing with foreign countries and foreign export can launder money in an even more convoluted way, making it virtually untraceable.

Laundering money serves two purposes: accounting for illegally gotten income and disguising it as legitimate, and financing other criminal enterprises. A new operation can be bankrolled by a "loan" from a cover company, and the personnel can be carried on the payroll of another company.

Whatever the actual use in a particular case, a "legitimate" business owned and operated by criminals is never legitimate. It is there to aid a criminal purpose even though many people would like to believe otherwise.

17. Finding The Targets

There are basically two avenues to finding targets used by vigilantes: active and passive. Each has its use, and in practice they often overlap.

a) Passive methods involve letting the target come within the vigilante's striking range. Guarding and stakeout operations are of this sort. Targets of opportunity are another example of passive targeting, in which luck brings an otherwise inaccessible target within reach.

b) Active target seeking is somewhat more common. Decoy traps fall into this class. So does active pursuit by a posse comitatus.

Active targeting means researching the target and then going out and finding him. Researching means getting adequate, accurate, and abundant information about the potential target, his activities and his defenses, his vulnerabilities and quirks. That is possibly the most challenging aspect of the vigilante's task, for it requires a lot of thought and there is little room for error.

The search for information will take up the next chapter.

18. Information

Developing accurate information is a specialty in itself, just as important to the vigilante as is the choice of tactics and weapons. In fact, only with information can an intelligent decision about anything else be made.

There are several sources of information available to the vigilante:

a) The News Media.

Often the media are how one finds out about a crime problem and its seriousness. While it is foolish to believe anything that can be read in the newspapers or appears on the six o'clock news, the media often give enough accurate information to enable the vigilante to make a start. One example is that of a neighborhood mugger. The media report that for the past several weeks a mugger has been operating in a certain locale. The number of victims is given, some statements by them, and perhaps a description. A victim may be quoted as to the mugger's method of operation. Based on this information, the vigilantes can make a decision as to how to approach the problem. They can decide whether to stake out the likely spots or whether to employ roving decoys. That decision depends in part on the layout of the field of operations, which can best be appreciated by a personal reconnaissance, which is another valuable technique of obtaining information.

A more tenuous way of using the media for information is to follow the investigative reporting articles. Often there will be an "exposé" of some racket or other, or some white-collar crime, in an effort to stimulate the police or the public prosecutor into action. Many times the "expose" appears, some statements are uttered by public officials, the matter is forgotten, and everything goes back to normal. Such exposes are a start in developing information about a potential target. The vigilante will recognize that the "expose" might be largely the product of the reporter's imagination and that trial by newspaper does not mean guilt. Still, the articles will often have valuable information that can be used to develop other, corroborating information.

In an article on price-fixing, for example, the vigilante will find the name of the company or companies involved and perhaps their addresses. In any event the addresses are not hard to find in the phone book. Also listed may be the names of the corporate officers who would have the authority to determine the prices, the outlets where the goods in question are sold, and statements by company officials.

A recent article in "The New York Times" told of an investigation into phony repairs by the Attorney General's Office and listed the garages which had performed spurious repairs and those who the investigation had cleared. The locations of the garages were listed along with the names.

A shopkeeper who is concerned about a wave of robberies and who bands together with other shopkeepers in his area to form a group to combat this problem will often be able to make valuable judgments from information available in the media. Sometimes it is very detailed, specifying, for example, the kinds of weapons carried by the robbers, the kind of car they drive, and even good descriptions. This can be invaluable if the merchants decide to form stakeout squads.

b) Personal communication. Interviews with victims or with witnesses are perhaps the best way of getting information about many types of targets. Direct contact permits questioning to disclose details that would otherwise remain obscure.

One vital point concerning interviews is that the vigilante cannot go around indiscriminately interviewing the victims of crimes or witnesses as if he were the police. That tactic is very heavy-handed and will quickly bring him to the attention of the police. There are certain procedures that will work if followed in the right situations.

If the vigilantes are shopkeepers who have been stimulated

to action because one or more of their number have been the victims of robberies will be no problem at all in getting information without being indiscreet. There will be no obstacle to getting complete co-operation from the victims.

Another situation is if the victim is a close friend, neighbor, or member of one's family. Eliciting information in these instances will be no problem.

Establishing legitimacy and gaining co-operation can be quite an obstacle if the victim is unknown to the vigilante. Any attempt can tip the vigilante's hand and alert the local police, and as we have seen, the police tend to be chronically hostile to anyone who threatens to do their job better than they. One approach is to conduct the interview by telephone, without disclosing identity. It might still alert the police that something is going on but at least the most vital information, the identity of the vigilante, remains secret. One such approach might go something like this:

"Hello, Mrs. Smith, I'm with the 23rd detective squad and just going over my men's reports on the robbery this afternoon. I need a few more details to fill in the picture. Can you give them to me?"

Impersonating the police is usually a felony, but if done discreetly over the phone will not get the vigilante in any trouble. It has been done successfully in person, but that does involve a definite risk, not the least of which is running into the real police.

If the victim has made a statement to the media and the tone of the interview leads the vigilante to feel that the victim feels not only hurt but outraged, that opens up a possibility of a direct approach:

"Hello, Mrs. Smith, I heard you on the six o'clock news when you said that you'd like to see the men who robbed you strung up. Did you really mean that?"

"Yes, I did. Who are you, anyway?"

"I'm someone who might string them up for you if I had a little more information that would help me find them. What we need now is some vigilantes and some friends of mine and I have decided to do something about it."

"But what can I do? I've already told all I know to the police. Won't they catch the robbers?"

"The police work their way and we work ours. If we can get your co-operation we'll be that much further in catching these men. It would also help if you didn't tell the police that we called, because they don't like private citizens doing their job. Can you help us?"

"All right. What do you need to know?"

Interviews with victims and witnesses are particularly valuable because the police customarily do not release all that they know to the media and often edit out some of the information before it is released.

c) Word of mouth. This is not quite the same as interviewing victims and witnesses, as we shall see. Often people have some knowledge of a criminal operation that is scanty or fragmented but which, when put together with other facts, lead to an adequate picture being built up.

One way this can happen is a casual conversation between two people who work in the same place:

Mr. A: "I got a good deal last week. My car was in a wreck, you know, and I took it to this place down the street and they told me that I could get the whole front end fixed with a front end from a used car and save some money. I said okey, they billed the insurance company for a grand, and I signed the papers and they gave me back a hundred right there."

Mr. B: "It looks like maybe the front end you got was from a stolen car. Didn't you ask?"

Mr. A: "No, I didn't ask. I don't care. All I wanted was to get the car fixed and now that I made some money on the deal I'm not going to rock the boat."

Mr. B: "Where is this place, exactly? I want to know just in case I get in a wreck."

Mr. B's neighbor's car was stolen last week and he suspects that it might have gone to a "chop shop" where stolen late-model cars are cut apart for spare parts. This is a start at finding out what happened to the car. A quick drive by the garage might reveal something interesting. If not, a visit to ask about getting a new engine for the year and model car of the sort his neighbor has might prompt some useful information. The garage owner might phone his supplier in Mr. B's presence. Knowing the number dialed might be a start to locating the place and if the reconnaissance shows the stolen car to be there the chain of proof is complete enough for the vigilantes to act.

Many Americans work for a company that employs dishonest practices, either directly or tangentially contributing to crime. The company that bribes a government inspector; the merchant who buys goods that he knows are stolen so that he may make a higher markup; the company that adulterates its products; all are part of the big crime picture that pervades the country. Additionally, some people are acquainted with known criminals. Some are related to them. All of these have information to give if they are approached and handled correctly.

The vigilante is not a professional interrogator; often he relies on luck. One such sort of luck is having a friend or a relative who is a law officer. He can provide much information that is not available to the general public.

Whatever the exact source, word-of-mouth can provide accurate and valuable information, as well as absurd rumors.

d) Informants. This is closely allied to, but different from word-of-mouth. An informant is a spy. Informants are usually widely used by the police, who do not have to fear discovery. If their "snitch" is discovered, it is he who will suffer the consequences, not they. On the other hand, a spy used by vigilantes could, if exposed, reveal the identity of his contact and that could be a very great danger for the vigilante.

In any event, informants are so rarely encountered in the vigilante field that they must be classified along with the factor of luck, something that one exploits when encountered but not to be relied upon.

e) Publicly available information. Under this category fall telephone directories, city directories, standard reference books that can be found in any library, and the like. Street and road maps are available almost everywhere.

These sources, while not revealing dramatic information

in themselves, often provide vital supplementary information for the vigilante.

f) Purloined documents. A vigilante who is contemplating committing serious felonies to enforce the law does not shrink from less serious ones, such as breaking and entering to obtain written information. Such might be found in an address book, for example. Another might be a file of receipts or of purchase orders for a business that deals in stolen merchandise.

Just as important as the means of getting documentary information is its evaluation. While it is no great task for a vigilante to read a phone number out of an address book, it does require some specialized knowledge to interpret business documents. Usually this is not a problem because the vigilante involved already has knowledge of the field.

A vigilante who finds it necessary to burglarize suspect premises to develop information will not be so unsubtle as to take only the information that he needs, leaving everything else intact. He will disguise the effort as a general burglary, taking cash and other valuables if possible. Otherwise, he will try to make it look like crude vandalism, destroying enough property to hide the fact that the primary object was the documents.

g) Police sources. The vigilante who is a policeman or who is in a group that includes a policeman in its number is lucky indeed. The police have available to them much information which is absolutely denied to the general public.

The policeman who is a vigilante can use:

1) Investigation reports. This is information "right from the horse's mouth". It is the raw meat of crime information that has not been digested by the media and very valuable.

2) Intelligence files. Depending upon his exact duties, the policeman may or may not have access to the department's intelligence files, which contain information on major crime figures and syndicates. This information looks mundane at first, and is often not the type that can support a prosecution or it would have already been used, but to a vigilante it can be invaluable. Some of the details contained in a file on a prominent criminal might be; addresses of various properties

owned, residence, lists of friends and relatives with their addresses, mistresses, the suspect's daily schedule, hobbies and interests, etc.

A vigilante interested in where a certain person would be at a certain time of day would find information such as this very helpful. It is information often developed from countless hours of surveillance and other means not readily available to the vigilante.

3) NCIC. This is the National Criminal Information Computer, located in Washington, D.C. and available to almost all police departments in the country. It can tell a suspect's criminal record and whether or not he is wanted anywhere in the country, as well as routine information such as Social Security number, date of birth, description, etc.

4) Word-of-mouth. Policemen talk, just as do other people, but what they have to say is not usually what other people say. Because of their calling, they are more aware of the crime picture and particularly of its less visible aspects, such as who is taking payoffs from the syndicate. Information on payoffs, in fact, can be the most valuable information a vigilante can acquire, as it gives him an opportunity to not only strike at a very vulnerable part of a criminal operation but to obtain financing for his own operations.

h) Surveillance. This can be the most rewarding and yet the hardest part of a vigilante's operations. Information developed through surveillance can provide the crucial breakthrough in a case and yet take weeks or months to acquire.

It is easy for a police department to assign detectives to "sit on" a suspect and report his every move. It is difficult for vigilantes, who have to earn their livelihoods and attend to families, to devote as much time to the task. The vigilante must compromise, must be ready to accept only partial results because he cannot sustain the effort that the task requires.

Surveillance is of two sorts, for the purpose of this discussion; physical and electronic.

Electronic surveillance involves placing bugs, recorders, and telephone taps. The fictional vigilante has all of these useful gadgets in his bag of tricks and he uses them often, but in real life that is not so. One of the obstacles is technical know-how. Another is access to the suspect premises, which may not be possible. Yet another is time. Anyone who has ever tapped a telephone or used a bug for real will know that most of the conversations intercepted are irrelevant and boring to listen to. Even the most flamboyant criminal in the country spends most of his day discussing what he will have for lunch that day, how much to tip the waiter, whether his car needs a tune-up, how much it cost to have his kid's teeth fixed, etc. That places a limitation on what can be picked up through electronic surveillance.

Another is that criminals are very much aware of the possibility of electronic surveillance and are very careful of what they say on the telephone. In fact, many of them are habitually circumspect and speak in only the most guarded and elliptical phrases, so that a casual listener will not really know what is being discussed.

Physical surveillance is more practical for the vigilante than is electronic, as it requires less specialized skill and no special access to possible guarded premises. It is more time consuming but the task can be divided among several members of the vigilante group. Physical surveillance will be covered more thoroughly in another chapter.

i) Interrogation. Interrogation, as distinghished from interviewing, is the questioning of hostile witnesses or suspects. For the purposes of our definition, interviewing is a gentle art, interrogation requires some forcefulness. Forced questioning of criminals is a common technique among vigilantes, and torture is accepted as a legitimate technique. This too, will be treated in a separate chapter.

19. Correlating Information

Collecting information can be hard work. Correlating it into a meaningful pattern is sheer drudgery. Researching out an individual or company from various sources takes a lot of time and effort and putting it all together takes even more. However, it is worth it. A couple of composite cases will illustrate the point:

A certain company has been disposing of stolen merchandise on the retail market. The vigilantes, before striking, do their homework. They look up the company's incorporation papers at the county office, and while thev are there they examine the records of the property. From this information they go to the city directory and a trade directory. After culling all of the important details and following up all of the leads the information developed includes:

A) The names and home addresses of the owners of the company, taken from the incorporation papers.

B) The name and address of the company's lawyer.

C) The name and address of a relative of the company president, which was gotten from the deed to his house. The house is co-owned. The relative lives elsewhere and if ever it is necessary to find the company president and he is not at home, the relative's address is one place to look.

D) The name and address of another company, dealing in car parts, some of whose stock is owned by the first company.

E) The name and address of its lawyer, which happens to be the same as that for the first company. This lawyer's name also appears on the house papers. He apparently does a lot of business with organized crime. A watch on his other clients might well be profitable.

F) The address of a warehouse in the suburbs jointly

owned by both companies. This is a valuable lead, as a watch kept on that warehouse might turn up some recently stolen goods.

G) The address of a house owned by the second company and lived in by its president. This is a commonly used tax dodge.

Another such case involved only an individual who was suspected of dealing in, but not using, drugs. He was known to have been born in a nearby city and the search started with the birth records, which listed his birthday, his parents' names, and their address. A search produced the names of two brothers born to the same parents at the same address a couple of years later. A look in the city directory showed that one person with the same name as one of the brothers lived there.

Going to schools in the area and looking in their yearbooks produced some results. A photograph of the suspect was gotten from a high school yearbook. A search of the city directories for previous years also disclosed where the suspect had worked during those years.

The suspect lived in a one family house and looking up the records provided the information that the house had been co-signed by a person who had a reputation as a gangland figure. The yearbook had listed skiing as a hobby of the suspect and a phone call to a ski club nearby showed that he was indeed a member and often went on skiing trips with them. In fact, he rarely missed an opportunity. This meant that some prediction could be made as to when he would be out of town, so that a search might be made in his house without fear of interruption.

20. Surveillance

Surveillance, for the vigilante, is at the same time more simple and more complicated than it is for the police. It is more simple because the requirements are looser: there is no need to obtain evidence which will hold up in court or to satisfy official requirements. It is more complex because the vigilante is not a full-time investigator with countless hours and an unlimited staff to throw into the effort.

There are two general types of surveillance; fixed and moving. There are several purposes to surveillance:

1) Locating a suspect.

2) Locate the suspect's residence, hangouts, friends, and criminal associates.

3) Get more specific information about a suspect's activities.

4) Cover a specific location used in a criminal activity and determine who visits it and why.

5) Obtain information as to the timetable of a particular suspect.

Fixed surveillance may be easy or difficult. It is easy to say: "Stake out that place." but it is another matter when it is necessary to find a location from which an inconspicuous surveillance can be maintained. The old cliche of two men in a parked car will often draw unwanted attention.

As a rule, a watch can most easily be maintained in a crowded area rather than an isolated and uncrowded one. In an urban setting, there are many places where a watcher can stay without attracting the wrong kind of attention. The vigilante can easily blend in with the crowd, whether he is watching or tailing the suspect.

There are three types of places from which a watch can be maintained: public, semi-public, and private. A public place is the street or a public building, including a restaurant or diner, or a theater.

A semi-public is a place open to the public but in which one can obtain some privacy, such as a hotel or motel room. A hotel room allows a lot of latitude in surveillance. The need for moment to moment alertness is less, as there is not as great a risk of discovery, and several watchers can gather to confer.

A private place is just that: private premises such as a house, apartment, or company. Sometimes the vigilante is lucky in that he happens to live or work near the place which he wants to watch. This is very convenient and very economical, as there are no hotel costs to pay. It is also very safe, as the vigilante has a legitimate and obvious purpose in being in that place, which almost eliminates the risk of exposure.

A moving surveillance, known as a "tail", means following the suspect to find out where he goes. This is most easily done in a crowded area, where the follower can blend in with the crowd. There are many sophisticated techniques of "tailing", but the vigilante cannot use them all. He is limited to what is called a "loose tail", which means following the suspect at a distance so as not to arouse suspicion and abondoning the pursuit upon the slightest sign that the suspect may be aware of being followed. The vigilante has to be prepared to compromise and to bank on being able to pick up the tail another time, as the risk of exposure is too great.

The suspect may decide to test for a tail by doubling back, by stopping and looking in shop windows, etc. The vigilante really cannot cope with this as he is not the police and has no official status. He must remain inconspicuous at all costs and risk failure rather than discovery.

Many times, however, the task of surveillance is not very difficult. It is easy to follow a truck in a city, for example. If the truck is the one that contains stolen merchandise, following it will perhaps lead to a warehouse where the goods are to be stored. Often, the driver is just a hired hand, unaware of the nature and origins of the goods he is ferrying and not, therefore, on the alert for a tail.

With criminals, their alertness often diminishes as they get further away from the scene of the crime. A car thief will be very careful while actually stealing the car, but the people at the "chop shop" to which he takes it may leave the car sitting out in the open for weeks, making no attempt to cover or disguise it, feeling that nodody can tell just from looking at a car sitting in a junkyard among many others that it is "hot".

Whatever the surveillance task, it usually will require three things from the vigilante: time, money, and guile.

Sometimes a surveillance task can last for weeks and go around the clock. Not many vigilantes have the resources in manpower to sustain such an effort. A schedule will be needed to cover the blocks of time and juggling the time of the individual members will be a complex, almost impossible, administrative task.

Money will be required to pay for motel rooms, meals, gasoline and carfare, and other expenses that crop up in a surveillance. If the expenses are small, the individual doing the surveillance may be able to pay for them out of pocket. If not, some provision must be made to supply him with enough money for the task. In some cases, money will be the limiting factor. Some tasks simply cost too much. An airplane ticket can easily cost a week's pay or more, for example.

The vigilante will want to, above all, remain unnoticed. He will blend into the crowd or into the background. He will have the guile to disguise himself and his purpose so as not to stand out and attract notice. Whether in the street or inside, he will be inconspicuous, wearing clothing that blends in with the type of neighborhood, driving an ordinary looking car, and making every effort not to make waves.

There are various manuals on criminal investigation which deal with surveillance in great detail. These, although commonly available, are of limited usefulness to a vigilante, who does not usually do things "by the book" anyway.

21. Interrogation

Interrogation is a means of obtaining information that is sometimes neglected by vigilantes in their haste to administer justice to the offender. It was not always so. Posses chasing criminal gangs in the Eighteenth and Nineteenth Centuries would routinely ask any members they caught for information concerning the whereabouts of the other gang members.

There are two differences between interrogation by the police and interrogation by vigilantes:

1) The vigilante is interested only in obtaining information which will help him carry out his plan against the criminals he is fighting, not in developing evidence that will stand up in court.

2) The vigilante does not have to read the prisoner his rights.

There may be an exception to this last point, in the event that the vigilante decides to turn his prisoner over to the police, but then he is not a vigilante in our sense of the word. Making the apprehension and depending on the police and the courts to administer justice is not vigilantism. The methods used may be the same, however, and that leaves a gray area that defies definition. Sometimes, in the event that the crime is not too serious and that one of the offenders is a juvenile, the vigilante may make an exception to his customary practice of summary punishment and give his prisoner to the police, or leave him where he will be found by the police. In such a case, it will be important not to take any action that might result in the suspect's being released through the effects of the Miranda Decision.

There are two broad areas of information of interest to the vigilante when conducting an interrogation: information as to the identities of other members of the criminal syndicate and their whereabouts, and the location and time of other criminal activities.

Sometimes vigilante operations do not permit any attempt at interrogation. If the action is such that a shootout is the inevitable way of deciding the issue there may well not be any prisoners left to interrogate. When staking out businesses that have been plagued by a series of robberies, for example, it might be difficult to take any of the robbers alive.

In any event, any prisoners taken should be immediately searched and restrained, if not with handcuffs, then with rope or wire. It can be troublesome to the interrogator if the suspect being questioned pulls out a weapon in reply.

Sometimes an operation can be mounted for the express purpose of capturing a prisoner for interrogation. This sometimes is called a "snatch job" and is, in effect, kidnapping. The basic technique is usually several men suddenly closing in on the suspect, immobilizing him, and carrying him off to a place where he can be questioned. This works best in an isolated area but it has been done successfully in a city, because passers-by rarely interfere when they see something such as this happening. The same people who stand by and watch an old lady get mugged on the street are hardly likely to have the initiative to obstruct a snatch.

A snatch job, to be done properly, should be done when the suspect has no friends or confederates nearby. He might be in the middle of a crowd; in a city he will be, but for the vigilante's purposes he will be alone. A good place for a snatch would be a parking lot or garage, for example. The suspect will be preoccupied in getting in or out of his car, and can be approached by several others without suspicion. The vigilantes who try to apprehend a suspect who is in his car with the engine running, however, might find it more difficult than they had anticipated.

A city street is also a good location. As noted above, the presence of bystanders is no problem, in fact if there are many people about they will obstruct the view of what is happening to those in the immediate area. This is a definite advantage if there are policemen in the area. The cop on the corner directing traffic will see only a sudden movement of bodies, a sudden stirring down the block.

Transportation to an isolated spot is the next step. As the vigilantes are concerned that someone may copy down the license plate number of any car they use, they have two workable choices: use a car that they have procured for this purpose and which cannot be traced to them, or use the suspect's car. Using the suspect's car is the easier route.

There are all sorts of locations suitable for interrogation and it is not necessary to go far out into the boonies to find one. The most important requirement is that it be out of sight and hearing. A basement anywhere will do well, as long as there is a stout door which will muffle any sounds of screaming. The back room of a shop after closing time, if there are no people nearby, will serve as well.

Part of the reason for the isolation is the psychological effect on the suspect. If he sees other people about, or hears them passing by, he will not get the feeling of total isolation that is so important in establishing the proper atmosphere for a successful interrogation.

The suspect must be made to feel that he is utterly isolated, that nodody knows where he is; that nobody will come to help him or even miss him until too late, and that he is completely in the power of the vigilantes. He must be convinced that his well-being and even his survival are in the hands of the vigilantes and that it is in his interest to keep them happy, which means of course, answering their questions.

It is not essential to be harsh or cruel to a suspect. Often the very situation, the feeling of isolation, will soften him up. Unfortunately, many vigilantes betray their amateur status by starting the session off with a beating. This is a waste of time, as a rule. In any event, the beating can always come later if the subject is uncooperative.

The mode of questioning is critically important. It is essential to remember that the suspect, if properly cowed, will be very cooperative. Sometimes he will be too cooperative and will tell the interrogator anything he feels the interrogator wants to hear. That is why it is essential to avoid leading questions. In any event, what the interrogator is trying to get is fresh information from the suspect, not confirmation of facts already known. This will make it easier to avoid leading questions.

Occasionally personality factors will impair the success of the interrogation. If the interrogator is the type who likes to play Gestapo he will risk spoiling it with his heavy-handed tactics. It is usually best to be low-key in manner, and persistence will be more rewarding than punishment. Asking questions in a calm and confident manner will work better than shouting.

The interrogator who starts by threatening the suspect is making a bad mistake. The most successful approach is a positive one. It will get better results to tell the suspect that after he has answered the questions he may leave rather than to threaten him with dire consequences for not answering.

If the suspect asks for little favors, such as being allowed a glass of water or to go to the toilet, straightforward refusal will only antagonize him and perhaps stiffen his resistance. It is better to tell him: "We'll get you something to drink after you tell us where they cut the heroin." Telling him something like: "You'll have yellow tennis shoes and a rusty zipper unless you tell me what I want to know!" will risk turning it into an endurance contest and will tend to mobilize his defenses.

The interrogator who asks a question that can be answered by a "yes" or "no" or by a shake of the head is making a cardinal error. That merely gives the suspect the opportunity to ascertain how much the interrogator knows and what he wants to hear. The interrogator holds all of the advantages here and he is foolish to give any of them away. An answer to a question that begins with; "who", "when", "why", "where", or "how" will always produce new information.

If the suspect is not cooperative at first, a useful tactic is to leave him by himself for a while, if that is possible. Time to think about his plight will tend to soften him up.

The vigilante who answers any question asked by the suspect is giving away his advantage. Replying in a way that does not tell the suspect anything he does not know already is the best way to answer. To the question, "Who are you?", the best reply is: "I'm just a guy who needs some questions answered." Another way is to answer a question with a question. That uses the suspect's spontaneity against him and in the interrogator's favor.

SUSPECT: "When will I get out of here?"

INTERROGATOR: "Where will you go when you get out?"

SUSPECT: "Out to a bar to get a drink."

INTERROGATOR: "Which bar?"

SUSPECT: "To the 308 Club, I guess."

INTERROGATOR: "Is that where you met Marroney?"

With this tactic the vigilante can get the best results out of difficult suspects. Sometimes, however, the suspect is very determined and some additional softening up must take place before complete cooperation can be obtained.

The difficult suspect is probably an experienced criminal and not a stupid one, either. Only outwitting him will work. It would be an insult to his intelligence to use the usual police tactics of Good guy-Bad guy, but a variation on the theme can produce the same result and enhance the effectiveness of the interrogator. The suspect will be exposed to several members of the vigilante group that has abducted him. These should be very firm, even abrupt, in their manner towards him. There should be absolutely no kindness or understanding displayed at all. By contrast, the interrogator should be a little warm and human. It is best if he not be a member of the snatch party at all because of the possibility of violence having been necessary to effect the kidnapping. The contrast in attitudes will tend to induce the suspect to relax in the presence of the interrogator, particularly if the others are not in the same room.

Should the suspect prove at all difficult, it will help if the snatch team occasionally make their presence felt. If the questioning goes on for several sessions the suspect will be given back to the custody of the strong-arm squad between sessions.

In the case of the especially refractory suspect who resists every effort to make him talk, the vigilante will use torture. Sometimes there is no other way. In such a case only the strongest measures will get results, and these measures are covered in the next chapter.

22. Torture

For centuries men have been practicing torture for various purposes. The methods have varied somewhat with the time and place, and some methods are considered to be obsolete. With the coming of the Twentieth Century new methods have been devised.

Torture has been so widespread that at least one book devoted to the history of torture has been published in recent years in this country. Today, more than ever, torture in its various forms is practiced throughout this country, as well as throughout the world.

The police and military use it. Sometimes they are squeamish about its use, and try to disguise the fact of its existence. Even the Gestapo called torture "Especially rigorous interrogation". The American police have called it "The Treatment" or the "Third Degree". Whatever the name, it is still as painful.

Some torture has been carried out using extremely complex methods that can only make one wonder about the mental stability of the persons who devised them. Others have been field expedients improvised on the spur of the moment from materials at hand. Vigilantes have to use expedient measures, as they have neither the time or the interest to invent exquisite methods of causing pain, and their resources are limited in any event.

Vigilantes, because of the nature of their endeavor, are not as limited in the use of torture as are the police. The police are obsessed with methods that will not leave marks which might show up in the courtroom. The vigilante has no such inhibitions and can be somewhat freer in his choice of methods. In fact, since many vigilantes wind up executing their captives, considerable lattitude can be allowed.

The interrogator will usually decide at the outset whether the torture will be designed to cause pain or to maim. Sometimes just a bit of physical pain, added to the anxiety that the captive is already experiencing, will induce cooperation. If he decides that causing pain will be enough, for the moment applying the measures will do with no further ceremony. On the other hand, if the tortures are those that will maim, such as removing an eye, the physical pain involved is usually no greater than that in other methods, and the psychological effect will be exploited. That means that the interrogator will explain in great detail what will be done before it is done, to let the suspect think about it and to feed his fear.

In some cases the decision will already have been made not to release the suspect after the interrogation. If the suspect knows this, the effect of the torture may be lessened, and the threat of maiming will be far less frightful, as he realizes that he will soon be dead, anyway. If the interrogator has been careful to tell the captive as little as possible all along and has been taking a positive line, ("after you tell us all about it you can go") the suspect will be unaware of this end and therefore more vulnerable. The threat can always be used: "How will you look to your family (or girlfriend, etc.) after we do this to you?" In some cases, the threat of castration will be particularly effective.

Modern torture methods can be very simple and take advantage of the materials at hand. There is no need for complicated apparatus, and in fact these are a liability, having more moving parts to get out of order. The simplicity of the method chosen makes it easier to apply and whatever equipment is required is more easily available. Some of the methods used in the Twentieth Century are:

a) Shallow cuts with an X-acto knife. These knives are commonly available and many substitutions are possible, such as a linoleum knife, paring knife, utility knife, etc., as long as the implement has a small and very sharp blade. The shortness of the blade limits the possibility that cuts made with it will be fatal and bring the questioning to a premature end. The point of the blade can be inserted under the fingernails, inside the nostrils, or the knife can be used to open up a number of shallow wounds all over the body. Naturally the suspect must be restrained before any cutting is done and care must be taken not to cut any major blood vessels, as this would cause premature death.

b) Needle-nose pliers are used for extracting teeth, fingernails, toenails, and hairs from sensitive parts of the body such as the pubic area and inside the nostrils. Pulling out eyelashes can be terrifying, although it is not very painful.

c) Larger pliers, such as the channel type, are useful for breaking fingers and toes by slowly bending them back against the hinge at the joint. They can also be used for extracting larger teeth.

d) Wire brushes are commonly available and can be used to scour sensitive and tender areas of the body.

e) Scouring powder of the sort used to clean toilets and sinks can be found in every home. A dash of this, particularly if it is the chlorinated kind, thrown into the suspect's eyes will cause intense pain that will be intensified by every movement of the eyes. Copious tearing will flush some of it out but a second dose can easily be applied.

f) Chlorinated water, found in every home, has been used effectively. A few ounces of this poured into the subject's nose and mouth will give the sensation of drowning in a particularly painful way. The old method used to be to put the subject's head down in a bathtub, force his head under for a minute or two, and then pull him out and revive him. Gradually, it came to be realized that gallons of water were not necessary: only a few ounces would do the trick, if poured into the suspect's nose and mouth. In fact, a person can be quite adequately drowned in a large bowl of water. The irritating effect of the chlorine enhances the distress.

g) Electricity causes pain when applied to any area of the body. If a cattle prod is available it can be used according to the manufacturer's directions. If not, the vigilante can easily improvise by taping a length of electric double-conductor wire to a short piece of broomstick, baring the ends and taping them to opposite sides of the end of the broomstick, and plugging in the other end of the cord. A nine-foot extension cord suitable for this use can be bought for as little as half a dollar on sale, even in these inflated days.

With a one inch gap between the ends of the wires, the broomstick can be touched to almost any part of the suspect's body to produce an encouraging response. Vigilantes will avoid the head and the trunk, though, for there is a risk of producing unconsciousness and convulsions if the current is passed through the brain, and if the current goes anywhere near the heart the interrogation might be cut short by the suspect's expiring from a heart stoppage.

A favorite area to apply the electricity is the genitals. Not only is the genital area very sensitive but many people have a lot of anxiety focused on their genitals, and the threat of castration or any sort of injury can force compliance from suspects who otherwise would be very tough cookies indeed.

h) Fire and heat. In popular fiction, more than in fact, we come across stalwart Allied soldiers having bamboo splinters inserted under their fingernails and set afire. This is done to them by the ardent interrogators of the Japanese Secret Police or by a Sadistic Japanese Submarine Captain, depending on the story. Nevertheless, fire and heat are very effective ways of making a subject talk when used with discretion.

The two commonly available implements for this purpose are the soldering iron and the butane lighter. Both produce more than enough heat: too much is undesireable because a severe burn destroys nerve endings, causing numbness rather than pain. Each has its advantages and disadvantages. The butane lighter is harder to control and is not likely to be carried by a nonsmoker and the soldering iron needs an electrical outlet nearby.

In use heat is applied much the same way as is electricity. Every part of the body is sensitive to burns and man has a built-in aversion to fire. Burning the fingers and toes while promising the subject that his genitals are next makes very effective use of both physical pain and anxiety.

Sometimes the torture will take on some aspects of "terminal care" in which the patient is not expected to survive. In such cases it can get very brutal and the interrogator must have a strong stomach and a lot of resolve to carry him through.

In some cases the suspect knows very well that he will be killed in the end and it might seem hopeless to try any psychological methods. The vigilante who is a good practical psychologist will know that a positive approach can still be made in such a situation. It is not necessary to throw away the carrot and just use the stick, even in the most extreme case. The subject can be approached with the promise of a painless death and an end to suffering. Emphasizing the positive aspect of it can gain more cooperation than endless torture.

It can be phrased euphemistically: "You can rest after you tell us what we want to know" or "Tell us about it and we'll let you sleep." Even when the sleep is the big sleep that comes out of the barrel of a gun the promise of it can be very effective to a person who is exhausted by pain, anxiety, and many hours of intensive questioning.

One problem that plagues vigilantes is the one of personality quirks. Some people become vigilantes not so much because of a serious dedication to law and order but because in this activity they can find expression for a streak of cruelty in their personalities: they enjoy thumping on people. Most of the time they have to be watched very carefully and even restrained, but sometimes they have their uses. When the situation calls for torture they come into their own. They can joyfully apply measures that would make other members of the group queasy and uneasy. It is a case of the right man in the right job.

23. Transportation

Often vigilantes need untraceable transportation. Using one's own car will do for routine purposes but for some surveillance and other tasks it can prove an embarrassment if a bystander happens to note the plate number. To avoid this risk when carrying out a "hit" or a "snatch", it is necessary to have a "cold" car or at least "cold" plates.

To a vigilante, a "cold" car is one that cannot be traced to him, directly or indirectly. This rules out not only personally owned cars, but rented and borrowed cars and company cars, if he is lucky enough to have one. All of these can be traced back with little effort.

There are several ways to procure a "cold" car for special purposes and the method the vigilante uses will depend very heavily upon his resources and the time available rather than upon a calculated choice.

a) Stealing a car is a fast way to do it but it is usually unacceptable to the vigilante because it puts him squarely in the same class as the criminals. This is a fine point in a vigilante's ethics which may seem hard to understand to the outsider, but breaking a technicality of the law is permissible to a vigilante, and so is committing a felony, as long as it is done to a lawbreaker. Injuring an innocent person is not.

Stealing a car, therefore, is something that will be done only in the most desperate situation, where it is a matter of survival.

b) Stealing plates. Many cars look alike: the unique distinguishing feature is the plate number. It is a simple matter to disguise a personally owned car by procuring plates from a car wrecking yard and putting them on. Some states have laws to the effect that all plates from cars to be scrapped must be turned in, but this law is not enforceable, particularly if the wrecked car is an out-of-state one.

Stealing the plates from a car that is being currently driven can lead to a serious problem: it will be reported and the police will have the plate number on a "hot sheet". Any attempt to use them can lead to being pulled over by a police patrol at the worst possible moment.

c) Confiscation. The difference between stealing and confiscating a car is that in confiscation the owner of the car is one of the criminals, not an innocent person. This can come about in several ways. Using the target's own car in the case of a snatch or a hit is the most common.

Another way is to maintain a list of cars owned by the targets or potential targets, and the places where they are usually to be found. When needed, a car can almost be stolen to order.

Confiscation on the spot, however, is the simplest method. It avoids the normal problems associated with stealing a car, such as obtaining the keys or forcing the ignition, storing the car until needed, the risk of having the victim report the loss, etc.

d) A second, "legal" set of plates for a personally owned car. This can be arranged in some states which are careless with their documentation. False I.D. can be generated and a set of plates procured with this. The procedure will vary from state to state and it is impossible to generalize.

e) Generating a totally "cold" car. This takes time and money. The basic procedure is to buy a car from an individual under a false name, paying cash to avoid the paperwork trail that a check or a credit card would leave.

One state in the Union issues license plates by mail to out-of-state residents, Alabama. With false paperwork it is possible to get genuine Alabama plates for a "cold" car. As this dodge is well-known to the police it has limited usefulness. Any attempt to use such a car on a regular basis between "jobs" could lead to a searching investigation if the driver is ever stopped for a traffic offense. Therefore, a "cold" car such as this is usually kept in cold storage until needed.

A sophisticated twist is to use the Alabama paperwork to obtain genuine plates in the state where the car is used. As a rule, no additional I.D. need be presented when applying for a transfer of a car, and it may be registered in-state with the false name and address on the paperwork. This method is about as foolproof as any can be, and it also costs a lot of money.

For the vigilante with enough time and money, it is possible to generate a totally untraceable car. The advantages are many, and the only difficulty is logistical.

24. Sanctions

Tradition has it that the subjects of vigilante action all ended up swinging from the end of a rope. This, like many other beliefs about vigilantes, is a myth. While capital punishment was often imposed, often it was not. Many times a beating was given, and in some instances the vigilantes did not take the subject into custody at all, but merely left a warning note nailed to his door. The one receiving the warning usually had to be out of town by sundown or face the consequences.

Death, of course, is the most dramatic and the most final sanction that can be imposed upon the criminal. Many vigilantes think of death first because they realize that they cannot impose an intermediate punishment, such as a prison sentence. In fact, history records a whole range of lesser sanctions that have been applied at one time or another. Death has been reserved for the most severe cases.

Many vigilantes of the past made a ceremony out of the administration of the death penalty. The group gathered with their prisoner around a stout tree, an announcement was made, the "condemned" was allowed to make a final statement, and then he was "executed", in a manner imitating the way the state did it. Today there is less room or time for this sort of quasi-legal ceremony. The end, for the criminal, is a quick bullet delivered right on the spot before he can say: "nolo contendere".

In many cases, the dividing line between a citizen acting in self-defense and a vigilante is that the vigilante has decided in advance that he will not turn the suspect over to the police but will execute him on the spot and plead self-defense, something which is easy to do when dealing with an intruder or a stick-up artist.

In other cases, the body of an organized crime figure is found in a ditch or the trunk of a car, trussed up and with a bullet in the brain. No clues exist as to the identity of the killer, and the police, in their statement upon the case, imply that not much effort will be made to find the killer. Reading between the lines, one can see that there are several good possibilities here:

a) The incident was merely a "gangland" killing by a professional killer who has left no trace and is long gone.

b) The gangster was done in by vigilantes, who are proving as elusive as professional killers. The police choose not to look too closely into the incident.

c) The killing was done by the police, in which case there is a police vigilante and the investigation will not be pursued with much vigor.

In all of these cases it is almost impossible to determine the immediate motive for the killing. Sometimes the police, through an informant, get a "rumble" that a certain person is out of favor with a mob leader and are not therefore, surprised when his body turns up in a few days. More often, there is no trace at all. The police are quite happy to sit back and enjoy the spectacle of mobsters murdering each other, and eagerly look forward to the start of a gang "war" which such a killing might spark.

If the killing has been done by a vigilante who is or is not a policeman, there is little point in pushing the investigation and the police act in a very circumspect manner because they do have more important crimes to investigate.

In fact, the police in many cases do have an abundance of things to occupy their time and will not waste much manpower investigating the death of what they consider one of the dregs of society unless they are motivated by an extraneous factor. Only if the killing is made to look like an affront to their competence will they get excited about it. That means, in practical terms, that a vigilante who kills his suspect and leaves a marksman's medal, or a similar talisman, beside the body is asking for trouble. The medal tactic is usually found in fiction, not in fact, and many fictional heroes have made it their trademark.

In real life, the vigilante is quite content to have the execution pass for a gang killing. If he is a policeman, he is doubly careful not to advertise. For these reasons, it is impossible to tell how many of the "gangland" killings of recent years have really been vigilante actions.

Sometimes one killing will set off a wave of killings. If one mob feels that a particular killing was committed by a rival mob, and do not accept a denial, then that starts a gang "war". Some of the gang "wars" of recent years may have started in exactly this way, with the vigilantes firing the first shot.

A lesser sanction that can be applied is corporal punishment. This is something that today is reserved for minor crimes such as vandalism. A group of citizens who band together in response to an epidemic of vandalism may choose to turn over any perpetrators they catch to the police. They may, on the other hand, decide to enforce the law themselves by flogging the vandal and then letting him go with a warning. If that is the course they choose they have crossed the line into vigilantism.

Corporal punishment is practical when the problem is severe but the act does not merit the death sentence or the offender is a juvenile. In fact, immediate punishment is likely to be more effective than the cumbersome machinery of criminal justice. The deterrent effect of knowing that punishment will be applied right on the spot is more real than the prospect of an arrest and being turned over to "juvenile" officers and being processed through "juvenile" court.

The main restriction to the use of corporal punishment is that it only works on petty offenders and amateur criminals. If it were tried upon a mob member it would probably lead to his coming back with some of his cohorts in search of those who had flogged him. The risk of being identified would be too great, as the hood would have only to remember the license number of a car to get a lead to the identities of the vigilantes, even if they all wore masks.

Destruction of property is a very effective sanction that can be applied to a variety of situations. It is easy, with little risk, because most of the property is unguarded most of the time and even alarm systems are only partially effective. An electronic alarm may impede burglars but it does not stop a gallon bottle of gasoline from coming through a window. In one incident in a small city in Arizona several years ago; a man who was the target of vigilantes had his house burned down in the early hours of the morning while he and his family were away on vacation. The building was isolated from other ones: there was no danger of the fire spreading, and the house was deserted, which assured that arson would not turn into murder. The man got the message and left town for good. The vigilantes, incidentally, did not leave a calling card or any indication that the fire was not an accident. There were no anonymous letters to the man or to the Fire Department and no medallions left at the scene.

Harassment is an increasingly common tactic today. It bridges the gap between overt felonious action and a warning. It is suitable for taking care of lesser offenders and some types of white collar criminals. Some methods of harassment are not illegal: some are in the gray area, and some are frankly illegal but have so little risk attached to them that they are very suitable for use by vigilantes.

Harassment is particularly suitable for use by the vigilante who is acting alone. The target has no way of knowing if he is being harassed by an individual or by a group and the effect is thereby enhanced.

A warning can be very effective, and in fact many times warnings were issued by vigilante committees, and the recipients were advised that they had twenty-four hours to get out of town or until sundown in other cases.

To be effective a warning must be credible. An anonymous note by itself will not have much effect. If, on the other hand, a vigilante group is known to be established and acting in the area, a warning purporting to come from this group will usually persuade the recipient to comply. More to the point, if there have already been examples of people who did not heed the warnings suffering dire consequences, then a warning will be very believable.

The modern vigilante has at his disposal a wide range of tactics with which to combat crime. Almost every day the media carry some of the ripples of the struggle. Much of it goes on below the surface because vigilantes do not advertise, for obvious reasons, and many vigilante actions are ascribed to other causes by the police, who are reluctant to admit that vigilantes exist.

25. Tactics

Just as the modern vigilante has the choice of a wide range of targets, because of the huge amount of crime that exists today, he has many choices as to tactics and their means of employment.

The basic decision is whether to go it alone or to form a group. Often this is not a conscious decision but it just "happens". The circumstances dictate the course of action in many cases. The shopkeeper or clerk who decided to keep a gun behind the counter is a good example. If he uses it just for self-defense against robbers he is merely doing what anyone would expect him to do in the circumstances. If he makes a conscious decision to kill the next person who tries to rob him, and call the police afterwards, he has crossed the line. However, his acting alone is not really of his own choosing; it is simply a fact that he will be alone when the robbers strike.

The lone vigilante is capable of the greatest flexibility. He acts alone: there is nobody with whom he must consult. If he has a change of plan he does not need to coordinate it with other members of a group. He enjoys the advantage of greater security than do the members of a group. The secrecy aspect is so important that it cannot be exaggerated, and the lone vigilante who is worried about a loose mouth has only his own to watch.

There are limitations to acting alone, however. The physical danger may be great, in which case the vigilante who chooses to act alone takes the greatest risk. Although the fictional hero of "Death Wish" is a very appealing figure, every time a vigilante goes out and uses himself for a decoy without any help he is laying his life right on the line and setting himself against the greatest odds.

The group has greater resources than the individual. Many of the problems of group action, solidarity, and recruitment are not very serious because of the way vigilante groups are formed. There are no advertisements in the help wanted columns saying: "vigilante wanted". Typically, a group of people who have known each other for a while decide, in the course of a casual conversation, to take action themselves. They have a common interest and they recruit each other. They are like-minded individuals and disagreements are minimal. They are all well-motivated and willing to give unhesitatingly for the common cause.

Such a group has a strength equal to more than just the sum of its parts. There is not only safety in numbers but a much greater effectiveness, whether the operation involved is a decoy, stakeout, or an active pursuit.

The members of a vigilante group, although gaining in psychological strength from their number, realize that there is no glamor in it for them, no glory. Their expenses will not be tax-deductible and if they are caught they will be in serious trouble. They will have to conduct their activities outside of their normal working hours unless they absolutely have to take a day off from work. Often the task will be boring and even unpleasant and the inner satisfaction of a job well done their only reward.

26. Weapons

Most vigilantes choose to be armed for their tasks, and considering the sort of people with whom they have to contend, this is understandable. The choice of weapons will be dictated by the task at hand, the tactical and legal considerations, and their own resources.

A major consideration is the status of the gun laws in the area. There are some places in this country where strict gun laws deprive the honest citizen of the right to own or carry a firearm, although they seem to have no effect upon the criminals. In such a case the vigilante may not have a gun at his disposal or if he does, it is illegal and its very possession will cause him grief if discovered.

It is usually possible to get a gun if one is really needed. Criminals do it all the time. This is an art in itself and often involves making contact with someone who already has a gun and purchasing it from him. The contact may be out of state, or he may be a criminal himself who deals in stolen property. Whatever the case, it is possible for the vigilante to arm himself in cases of dire need.

Another way for a vigilante to procure a firearm is to take it by force from a criminal. This is not always possible and it is very dangerous. It usually requires a decoy or a stakeout if a particular individual is not selected. When the robber or mugger strikes an attempt is made to disarm him. Apart from the great danger in trying to disarm a criminal, there is the complication that the vigilantes have to take pot luck in the choice of weapon. Another way to obtain a weapon is to ambush a person who is known to carry a gun. This is not as improbable as it might seem. Even in cities with the strictest gun control laws the biggest criminals often are able to obtain gun permits while respectable citizens cannot. They, their associates, and their bodyguards all have to move around, go shopping, go home, etc. They are not always on their guard. There are opportunities for ambushes, particularly when one such bodyguard is off duty on his way home, and perhaps thinking more of a warm bed and a warm body than alertly scanning his surroundings.

In such a case a typical urban ambush can be set up. It is very easy to get close to an unsuspecting subject in a parking lot or in an elevator and knock him unconscious with a blackjack.

If there is a choice of firearms the decision has to be made in terms of the situation and what is available. Between them, the members of a vigilante group are likely to have several types and calibers at hand, and something to suit almost every tactical requirement can be scraped up. If not, the members can chip in to buy it, in most cases.

A compromise usually has to be made between firepower and concealability. In fixed operations, such as stakeouts, there is usually room to stow something reasonably powerful such as a shotgun. For mobile actions, such as a decoy or an assassination, it might not be possible to carry anything bulky unless a vehicle can be worked into the plan and kept close by.

In the typical urban operation the vigilantes cannot walk down the street with guns showing, as a line of men stalking through a neighborhood like an infantry patrol is likely to provoke a phone call to the police. It is necessary to conceal the weapons and yet have them easily available, for the sake of surprise. For this reason, a coat pocket will turn out to be much more useful than the most expensive holster. Another way to carry a weapon so that it is always available but out of sight is in a paper bag. The sight of a man walking down the street carrying a paper bag is not as alarming as that of a man with both his topcoat and jacket open on a cold day, with his hand hovering inside his coat.

In decoy operations, the spectacle of a man stalking the streets with his hands in his coat pockets, in "Death Wish" style, is more likely to put off a suspect than that of a man or woman struggling with one or two grocery bags. This is where fact contrasts with fiction.

In many cities, there are laws against carrying loaded firearms within city limits and if there is danger of a search by police the vigilantes have to be very careful and discreet. It is sometimes wise to forego the advantage of a firearm in favor of a weapon that is not so obvious and that is not prima facie evidence if discovered. A ball-peen hammer is a good choice for a vigilante because it certainly is deadly if properly used, yet it is an ordinary tool. As an impact weapon it is versatile because the ball end of it can be driven through the skull yet if the flat is used the effect can be restricted to stunning the suspect.

If the locale is such that weapons laws are strict and strictly enforced, the plausibility of the weapon has to be considered. A person who is a carpenter by trade can easily carry a hammer without incriminating himself: a plumber can carry a wrench. A tire iron can serve very well, particularly if it is used in a decoy operation in which the decoy plays the part of a standard motorist. In other cases it will not be possible to use impact weapons but the vigilante need not be unarmed and defenseless.

Certain products available in any supermarket can serve as weapons. Spray cans of oven cleaner, insecticide, or paint will incapacitate an assailant at close range. Every ghetto resident knows this, and many of them carry such a spray can with them. Such weapons fit easily into a grocery bag and indeed, can be bought just before the start of an operation if necessary.

If the preference is still for impact weapons a small sweeping brush can be used for striking although it is not as heavy as a blackjack. A bar of soap in a sock will crack a skull if swung hard enough. In some locales, with the police overtly hostile to vigilantes or anyone who tries to defend himself against criminal enterprise, weapons which are not obvious are the methods of choice.

An excellent discussion of everyday objects that can be turned into weapons is to be found in the book: "Invisible

Weapons" by Harold Jenks and Michael Brown, (Desert Publications, 1979).

One weapon which is very rarely used, contrary to what many think, is the silencer. The silencer is not adaptable to many firearms, it is cumbersome and makes the gun harder to conceal, and it does not work very well. Yet the popular image of the assassin firing at his target with a gun that emits soft pops lingers on in fiction and fancy.

The silencer will not work on a revolver or on a rifle, or any firearm that fires the bullet at supersonic speed. Typically it is a bulky affair, with the most effective ones being about a foot in length and the diameter of a salami. The vigilante worried about concealability will not have an easy time with such an apparatus. The silencer's effectiveness is much exaggerated — it should not be called a silencer at all but perhaps a sound softener. It does not reduce the sound of a gunshot to a whisper and anyone who claims that it does simply has not heard one in action.

For the vigilante, a situation that makes the silencer's added bulk acceptable would also allow more tolerance of noise. In fact, the easier it is to use a silencer, the less he needs it. One little noted fact is that, in the peculiar circumstances of a vigilante action, the target's body makes the best silencer of all. If the weapon is an automatic pistol, in which all of the powder gases go out of the end of the barrel (revolvers leak some between the barrel and the cylinder) pressing the end of the barrel hard against the target's body ensures that the gases will go into and be muffled by a body cavity. This produces an almost noiseless shot, as the mass of a human body can absorb a great amount of kinetic and acoustic energy. As most vigilante actions take place at very close ranges this is a practical method to use.

27. Gunfighting For Vigilantes

Many street criminals can be expected to be armed: despite this, they are not usually expert shots, otherwise the slaughter of policemen in shootouts would be a common thing. In fact, the police win almost all of their gunfights. This is significant in view of the fact that most policemen are not particularly good shots themselves, still, the hoods are worse.

In a gunfight, being a marksman is not as important as being a good tactician. For the vigilante the advantage of surprise is equally important.

Many "experts" sincerely advise the citizen faced with an intruder or a stickup man not to try to resist. They reason that the criminal is armed and ready to use force and that it is extremely dangerous to try to fight him on his own ground. What is really significant in such a situation is the advantage of surprise. The citizen who is genuinely taken by surprise is at a great disadvantage. The vigilante, however, is not.

In armed confrontations the vigilante will be either the aggressor or the counter-aggressor and will not be caught at a disadvantage. If he is the aggressor it will obviously be the criminal who is taken by surprise. If he is the counter-aggressor, as in a stakeout or decoy situation, he might be taken by surprise tactically, as he cannot predict the exact moment the criminal will strike, he is ready for it and prepared to react forcefully. The contrast between the armed and determined vigilante and the sleepy householder who is awakened in the middle of the night by noises coming from the kitchen is a very significant one and the difference in their combat effectiveness is very great.

The vigilante can plan his course of action, even if his basic tactic is to wait for the criminal to come to him. He will have already assessed the situation and decided what he will do and when he will do it. He will perhaps have help from others who are concealed nearby. The vigilante is ready for trouble when it strikes and more to the point, he is ready to give the criminal trouble.

In a vigilante action, as in other types of gunfights, the object is to win, not to dazzle the enemy by displaying remarkable feats of shooting skill. As the vigilante is out to win and determined to get a sure hit, he will attempt to stack the odds in his favor. That means arranging the situation so that he almost can't miss. As most vigilante actions, particularly on the asphalt frontier, will occur during the hours of darkness it is particularly important to shorten the range at which shots are fired to improve the prospects of a hit. Ideally, in an attack from the front, the range should be just out of touching distance, about five feet, to prevent the target from reaching out and deflecting the gun muzzle or trying a disarming tactic. From the rear shots should be fired at contact distance for a sure hit. Pressing the muzzle of the gun into the target's body is the best way of ensuring a hit. It has the added advantage of muffling both the sound and the muzzle flash.

There are several ways of disarming a person who holds a gun. These all depend on being within touching distance and on having the time to determine exactly where the gun is. In the event the person holding the gun has made the decision to shoot as soon as he is lined up, there is almost no opportunity for unarmed defense except for a reflexive strike at the gun muzzle if the attack is made from the front. The vigilante has the advantage, therefore, of knowing what he is going to do and of not allowing his target any time to effect a countermove.

In outright aggressive action, such as an assassination, the vigilante does not need to concern himself with the problem of cover as much as in other situations, as he has the advantage of surprise. However, in the case of a stakeout, where the tactics can be planned well before the action starts, the vigilante can assess the area of operation to select firing points that give good cover as well as good fields of fire.

Cover is particularly easy to find in urban situations because of all of the structures surrounding. the field of action, but it is also possible to mistake concealment for cover and to suffer from the mistake. Many interior walls will not stop anything more powerful than a B-B gun, and the vigilante who takes up a position behind one of these without using additional protection will be vulnerable.

An interior wall is almost as flimsy as cardboard, but a piece of solidly built furniture in front of or behind it will enhance its resistance to penetration of bullets. If there is time for detailed planning and extensive preparation, a piece of steel plate can be employed as armor. This will stop almost anything, depending on the thickness of the steel. Mild steel one quarter of an inch thick will stop handgun bullets and a half-inch thick piece will stop most rifles.

In a typical vigilante action the object is not to take prisoners but to shoot first and to keep on shooting until the criminal is dead or incapacitated. This is why the vigilante will tend to overkill, that is to shoot until the criminal is a bloody hulk on the floor or until he runs out of ammunition. Because the object is not capture but execution, he can feel free to use all the firepower he feels necessary.

In the event that the suspect is still alive the vigilante will most likely administer a "coup-de-grace", a last killing shot. This is usually delivered in the head for an assured clean kill.

Specific gunfighting tactics are chosen to suit the situation, and in the following chapters we will cover how the police handle some types of situations and how the vigilantes do it, and the reasons for the different approaches.

28. Assassination

The traditional "necktie party" is rarely seen nowadays and for the best of reasons: it is obsolete. Hanging is a clumsy and inefficient way of disposing of someone and there are often embarrassing problems such as the target's not dying immediately but lingering for many minutes which are almost more painful for those watching than for the condemned.

Hanging requires a precise calculation by formula of the length of the drop, in order to break the neck and cause immediate unconsciousness and death. Often, the formula does not work, because of individual differences in weight, build, and musculature. Then the hanged person either lingers on or falls so far and so fast that the head is sheared off.

Execution by the gun is an excellent method. It is fast, easily performed, and requires no exotic skill to carry out. It can be done anywhere, not just in the proximity of a tall tree or a lamp-post. It is not as ceremonial, which will be a disappointment to some, but the whole idea of an old-fashioned killing ceremony is out of step with the Twentieth Century, despite state-run executions that are almost medieval in their ceremonial aspects.

The usual pattern is for the vigilantes to accost the target when he is alone in an isolated place and to shoot him to death as quickly as possible. There are many variations to this form, and we will take a quick look at some of them. Starting with the simplest, we have:

a) The simple kill. This is performed by as little as one vigilante, as it does not require a complicated operation or coordination with others. The target is approached when he is in some sort of isolation, such as a parking lot or garage, or in an elevator, and killed. The method of killing can be a gun, and in many places the noise will pass unnoticed, or it can be a knife or a bludgeon. A hammer is a very effective tool for this, as it is cheap easily procured, and easily disposed of after the event. There is no warning given - the target is simply approached and killed before he can become suspicious or react.

In fiction, a talisman is sometimes left by the body. In real life, this is rarely done, as it would just call attention to the vigilante and this is something which the vigilante does not want. The assassination may even be disguised by stealing the target's wallet and valuables to make it look like a cheap mugging that culminated in death.

b) The planned ambush. A simple kill falls into the category of ambush and often it is planned, but it is a relatively unsophisticated affair. A situation in which the target has a bodyguard or two, or is assumed to be armed, is another matter. It requires definite planning and cannot rely on luck for success. The vigilante who decides to carry out an ambush will need to know about his target's movements to plan the best time and place for the execution.

The method chosen may be more complex than simply shooting or bludgeoning the target. The situation might be such that the best method would be to crush the target's car with the target in it, by means of a big truck, bulldozer, etc. Difficult situations require ingenious solutions.

If the target has a bodyguard or two, enough firepower must be available to neutralize them immediately, and every effort is made to attain surprise so that the firepower goes in only one direction. With all that, it is rare to see a full-scale shootout in the streets. There is too much danger to passers-by for the vigilantes to stage an ambush in any sort of public place unless there is reasonable assurance that it will be deserted. Sometimes it is possible to arrange for an assassination in a public place, such as a parking lot at three in the morning. One such effort might be arranged as follows:

Figure 1 shows the layout of a parking lot which has been chosen as the site of an attempt on "Mr. Big", the notorious mobster, A, B, and C are the vigilantes and each is positioned behind the engine compartment of a car to obtain

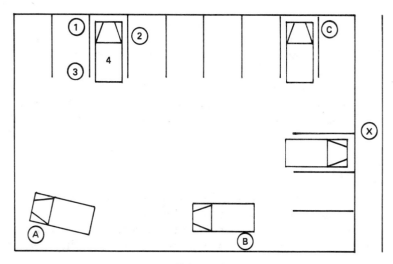

Figure 1

maximum cover. 1, 2, and 3 are the mobsters, who are approaching their car, 4. None of them can return fire effectively because when the shooting starts they are all in the open and the vigilantes are all under cover. C is particularly well placed to deliver cross-fire, which in this case means shooting behind whatever cover would be available to the mobsters. This prevents mobsters 1 and 2 from taking a quick step and getting behind car 4 and obtaining the protection not only of the engine but of its entire bulk. While A and B cover the front and sides, C covers the rear and the mobsters have absolutely no cover. In addition, car 4 has been disabled before the mobsters got there so that if one of them were still able to drive, he could not get away by driving out of there.

The cars behind which A and B are taking cover are positioned so that they are facing the exit, for a quick getaway. They can be started up quickly and driven out with a minimum of delay. There are two getaway cars as insurance against one of them being disabled in the firefight. In the event that both of them are, an alternate route of escape is planned, down alley X to a subway station a block away.

Sometimes an assassination requires more planning because it is not practical to execute the target right on the spot where he is found. He might be needed for interrogation, or it might not be feasible to kill him right there because of the risk to bystanders. In that case it is necessary to plan a "snatch".

c) The "Snatch". This is purely and simply an abduction and it is feasible only if the target is alone or has at most one bodyguard. There are two possibilities: The target has a car or he is on foot. If he has a car the vigilantes will follow him until the appropriate moment, crowd into the car with him, and overpower him and drive away. Firearms are not usually used.

An excellent moment for a snatch is when the suspect is getting into or out of his car. Then he is not as alert and is easier to approach, particularly if the locale is a parking lot or a garage, where he would expect to see other people around.

If the suspect is on foot, then the vigilantes must provide the transportation. A team is usually required for this. The best place for such an abduction is from the sidewalk because a car is only steps away, and the suspect need not be transported on foot for any great distance. The vigilantes usually choose a large car, not only for passenger capacity but for easy access. Generally, there are several men detailed for the snatch. The driver stays in the car while the others step out next to the suspect and take him. They may choose to alight further down and walk toward him, grabbing him at the last moment before they reach where the car is waiting.

The actual tactic for the abduction is approximately as follows:

The vigilantes surround the suspect and before he knows what is happening, they grab each of his arms to prevent him from either escaping or reaching for a weapon. If the suspect is known to be armed or particularly dangerous, one of the vigilantes will stun him with a blackjack to minimize the possibility of resistance.

Two points are critically important here: One is the absolute necessity of having enough muscle power at hand to overcome resistance and to physically lift the suspect, if necessary, into the vehicle. Manhandling is a definite part of an abduction. The other is that the suspect is stunned by a blow to the head if he is in the least recalcitrant. The fiction writers love to use drugs injected into a vein to render a subject unconscious and a couple of generations ago a chloroformed pad over the face was the method most often described, but nothing works as quickly as a blow with a blackjack or a rabbit punch.

For the occasions when the subject has a bodyguard, it is necessary to put him out of the picture right as the main effort begins. This requires an extra man who need not be a part of the snatch team itself and who, surprisingly enough, can make his getaway on foot, blending into the crowd as the people are watching the events by the car.

When properly done, a street abduction takes about five seconds or less. Passers-by have little or no opportunity to intervene and it happens so quickly that descriptions will be scanty.

d)   The bomb. This is not worth much discussion because it is such an imprecise method. It is all too easy to kill or maim the wrong person with a bomb and it is mainly the weapon of hoodlums and psychopaths, not vigilantes.

e)   The sniper. This method, though not very common, is known to work well when properly applied. By sniping, the vigilantes can cut through a screen of bodyguards. Kill the target, and get away with minimal risk to himself.

There are two main ways for a sniper to get at his target: at home or away from home. It almost never happens that a sniper can approach his target's home undetected, get close enough to assure a kill, and get a clear shot at him. The target is on familiar ground and the approaches are well covered. If he has bodyguards they are aware of the dangers, if they are at all competent, and any vantage points will have been either well covered or removed.

Away from home offers tne best prospects, and it is a fact that most people who have been killed by snipers have been shot away from home. The unfamiliar surroundings, the impossibility of controlling all points overlooking the target, and the sheer complexity of the buildings in the surrounding area make it almost impossible to protect against sniping.

It is a common misconception that snipers take shots at impossibly long ranges and unfailingly hit their marks. This simply is not true. A quick look at the recent sniping incidents (for the purposes of this discussion both vigilante and non-related snipings will be used) reveals that in all cases the range was under one hundred yards. Even in the remarkable assassination of President Kennedy the first shot was fired at a range of just under sixty yards, although it opened up rapidly as the car was moving.

Snipers tend to use telescopic-sighted rifles of medium caliber. This makes the most of the sight picture and minimizes the effect of extraneous factors such as wind. When it is considered that it is possible to hit a target the size of a man with a pistol at a hundred yards, the advantage that a telescopic sight and a rifle offers are obvious.

Typically, the sniper fires from concealment and from a rest. Cover is not critical, as he has finished the job and is gone before the target's escorts are able to determine from where the shots have come and to react.

Most of the time the target is not moving when shot. A moving target is more difficult to hit and the sniper seeks to give himself every advantage he can. He carefully selects a point that will overlook a site where the target will be still, or will stop during a journey.

The characteristics of the site are critical to the sniper's getaway, as well as to his success. He picks one with not only a good overview but a good clear escape route. In the city this means a building with an entrance on another street. In a rural area, he picks a sniper's nest with access from another road. That way he ducks out of sight immediately after firing and he does not reappear at all as he gets away. After the shooting everyone's attention will be directed to the events on the next street or the next road, and he can leisurely walk away from the scene, blending with the crowd if there is one, until he reaches his car, which he drives away slowly and inconspicuously.

f) Vehicular homicide. With all of the attention being focused on guns, many people are unaware of the number of killings done with an automobile. Even the police have little or no idea of the number.

It is a fact that, except for the motive in the driver's mind, the hit-and-run accidental killing is indistinguishable from the deliberate one. It is also more difficult to prevent a vehicular killing than most other kinds. An alert and perhaps suicidal bodyguard can forestall an assassination attempt with a weapon by interposing his body between the vigilante and the target, but if the attempt is made with a car, it will do no good. The most that a bodyguard can do is to try to push his client out of harm's way, but this does not always work and can be forestalled by wise choice of site.

Objectively, there is no way of telling how many suspects have been dispatched by motorized vigilantes. It is a certainty, given the circumstances, that the number is greater than anyone suspects or can prove.

The method is very appealing because cars are such a common part of life today and motor vehicle accidents are so frequent. Literally every day someone dies in a car accident. The car as a weapon is easy to use. It is easier to aim than a gun. It is, despite its size, less conspicuous. It makes less noise. Not only is it the weapon: it is the means of escape.

29. Intruders And Hold-ups

For the householder, store owner or clerk, or business-man the difference between practicing normal self-defense and becoming a vigilante is the conscious decision that any intruder will be dealt with on the spot rather than turned over to the police. The dividing line between self-defense and do-it-yourself justice is so thin as to be imperceptible in some cases.

For the householder and the store owner the decision is relatively easy. For the clerk or other employee, another decision has to be taken first. The store clerk may legitimately ask himself what is the point of resisting a robber. He may feel, with a lot of justification, that it is poor judgment to risk his life resisting a robber to defend someone else's pro-perty. Many people feel this way and it is hard to blame them, particularly if they are poorly paid.

Once the decision to resist is taken, it is only a slight step to decide not to take any prisoners. The store owner who shoots first is on legally unassailable ground in most of the fifty states. In some locales, such as New York City, defen-ding oneself with an unregistered gun becomes Murder One if the robber is killed. This is due to a technicality in the law stating that any killing committed while committing a felony is automatically First Degree Murder, even if the felony is a passive one such as possession of an unregistered firearm. Several people have been prosecuted for this and it is an object lesson for those who think that gun control.laws are good things to have.

For the householder and the store owner both, the action will start with them in a bad posture; that of tactical surprise. The store owner will certainly not have a gun in his hand

when the robber comes in and the householder will almost
certainly be roused from sleep and not be at his best, although
he may have a gun close by. The householder will find a
discussion of defensive tactics in a book called "Shotgun",
published by Desert Publications, Cornville, AZ.

The storekeeper has a different set of problems. The
typical hold-up comes down like this: The robber walks in,
posing as a customer, and browses around waiting for the
store to empty out. He does not feel comfortable announcing
a stick-up in the presence of others because they are a complicating factor. One of them might be an off-duty policeman.
Another might get hysterical or try to "play hero". In any
event, more people in the store means more people to watch
and control while directing attention to the storekeeper and
taking his money. The storekeeper verbally agrees to comply
with the robber's demands and either takes the money out of
the cash register or moves aside so that the robber can have
access to it. Only the robber who is in a great hurry or who is
very inexperienced will tell the shopkeeper to reach anywhere
for anything - he might come up with a gun. If there is a gun
in the cash register the robber takes it with him, for several
good reasons. If the robber flees without finding any gun, the
shopkeeper retrieves the gun from where it was hidden and
fires at the fleeing felon. Sometimes he hits and sometimes he
doesn't.

Analyzing the foregoing situation points up the following
conclusions:

a) The robber has the initial advantage, as he initiates
the action.

b) Both the robber and the shopkeeper have an interest
in having the premises empty when the action starts: the
robber so that nobody else will interfere, and the storekeeper
so that no innocent people will be in the line of fire when the
shooting starts.

c) The storekeeper will be wise not to keep a gun in the
cash register or drawer, or in any obvious place, such as a
shelf behind the counter.

d) A pistol is best kept concealed on the person: that
way it is close to hand wherever the robber tells the shop-

keeper to go. A shotgun is best kept in a closet in a back room, or behind a curtain.

e) There are two critical moments for a shopkeeper: when the robber first announces himself and decides whether or not the shopkeeper is complying satisfactorily with his demands, and when he is about to leave and is putting his weapon away, looking outside, and preparing to try to blend in inconspicuously with the outside traffic.

f) Either one of these can be the moment of decision for the vigilante. If the robber displays a knife and is out of immediate reach, the shopkeeper can draw and fire right away. When the robber puts his gun away, before he goes out and mingles with the innocent people on the street, he is vulnerable and the shopkeeper vigilante can open fire if he is careful to watch the background so that wild shots do not hit innocent people.

g) Another critical moment can occur during a walk-in, which is unpredictable in the sense that it might happen at any moment and anything might happen as the outcome. A customer walks in during the robbery. A policeman might even walk in. The customer might just come in, or he might react quickly, slam the door, and run away before the robber can react. The robber might shoot the newcomer in a panic. Whatever happens, it offers the shopkeeper a precarious chance to turn the situation around. He may elect to jump behind cover and shoot it out right on the spot. He might run out of another exit and wait for the robber to come out.

h) Other factors can intrude to tip the odds against the storekeeper: there might be more than one robber, or the robber might immobolize the storekeeper by tying him up or handcuffing him before leaving. He might lock him in a closet.

The diagram which appears at the top of the next page shows a composite of a store hold-up, illustrating various tactical principles. Not all of the features shown will automatically be found at the site of any one robbery. However, all of them have been involved in one robbery or another at various times and most are common to the average urban small retail store.

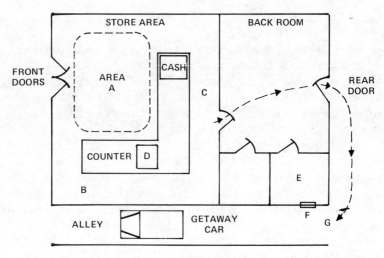

Figure 2

Not all of these features will be found at the site of any one robbery: all of them have been involved in one robbery or another at various times.

Area "A" is the likely area the suspect will be occupying during most of the time he is in the store. The front of the store consists of glass windows. The storekeeper will be at position "B" at the outset. The robber tells him to move away from the cash register and to keep his hands in the air. Item "D" is a display that has been purposely put there to serve double duty as a firing cabinet made of material thick enough to stop bullets.

If the proprietor can ease down near to this display he can draw and open fire while the robber is preoccupied with looting the cash. The walls are of solid masonry and there will be no danger to people outside, as there would be if the firing were in the direction of the glass front.

Position "B" is a place from which to fire if the robber is about to leave and is near the doors. The masonry side wall still serves as a backstop for the bullets. Under no circumstances should the proprietor fire from behind the back counter, as the danger to people in the street would be acute.

Position "B" has a piece of steel plate built into the counter, out of sight, as protection for the shopkeeper.

If the proprietor is behind or near the side counter when a walk-in occurs or the robber is otherwise distracted, he can immediately duck and fire. If he is at the back counter he can run through the doorway into the back room, where he has several choices. Anticipating pursuit, he can go to the closet where a shotgun is hidden, retrieve it, and wait for the robber to come through the doorway. The back room, having no windows except the one in the toilet, is safe for shooting. Another choice is to go right out the back door of the shop and flee for help. Yet another possibility is to go to position "G", taking cover behind the wall and waiting for the robber to come out of the back door.

The importance of adequate cover in the front of the store cannot be over-emphasized: neither can the importance of denying cover to the robber. Area "A" is clear of any displays that can serve as bullet-proof shelters. There may be a cardboard stand or two, but nothing solid in the robber's immediate area. This is particularly critical if there is more than one robber. A shootout against odds is made somewhat more attractive if the opponents are out in the open. In the same way, the area immediately around the door connecting the front and the back areas of the store is devoid of anything that could serve as cover: anyone coming through it is vulnerable to fire from someone standing behind the door near the closet, and cannot return the fire effectively because that is the hinge side of the door.

The robber may lock the proprietor in the closet in preparation for the getaway, most likely without checking to see what is inside the closet. The proprietor, having foreseen this, has equipped the closet with a lock that can also be opened from the inside. The toilet is the same way. As soon as the robber is out of the room, the storekeeper comes out and goes out the back way, waiting at position "G" for the robber to pass the alley. There is a certain risk to passers-by at this point and the shopkeeper may refrain from firing if there are many people on the street. He may choose to get into his car and shadow the suspect to a less crowded area.

He might have been robbed before, and noted that the suspect kept his getaway car parked in the alley facing the street during the attempt. On the possibility that the suspect might do this again, he can station himself at position "G" and wait for the suspect to approach the car, at which time he fires. Another possibility is to fire from the window of the toilet. This might be necessary because there might not be time to run out to the alley.

The hardest part is for the shopkeeper to decide to offer resistance to the robber. Deciding to impose the death sentence oneself is easy, and the effort required is minimal. The difference between disabling and killing is only an extra pull on the trigger, and sometimes not even that.

30. Decoy And Stakeout Operations

Decoy and stakeout operations are so similar in many ways, having so much in common in their planning and tactical concepts, that they must be dealt with together. There is more technique, finesse, and subtlety required for these than for any other type of operation that the vigilante is likely to undertake.

The police use decoys and stakeouts a lot and their methods are worth close study, as the vigilante will be operating in basically the same way, but with certain significant differences.

In both decoy and stakeout operations the enforcers are the watchers and even the potential victims of the expected crime. The danger is extremely high and the task involves many hours of alert inactivity which may explode into a violent encounter at any moment.

With the police the operation follows a set and predictable pattern. The police always operate in teams, sometimes just a pair but more often three or more. When operating a decoy one officer will be the decoy itself and two or more will be nearby as "backups", ready to come to his aid when required.

The decoy is an officer who tries to look attractive and vulnerable to the potential criminal. This involves more than changing from uniform to civilian clothing. The decoy can be either a female police officer or a male officer in disguise. In a campaign against rapists, for example, it is mandatory that the decoy give the appearance of a female but if operating against robbers or muggers it doesn't matter as much. Either sex will do as long as the decoy looks vulnerable and weak.

The disguise usually does not involve much makeup but rather role playing and a conscious attention to detail. Shedding the uniform is only the beginning. The officer must also stop looking and acting like a cop. He must not seem to be alert, must not be constantly glancing around him, checking out the passers-by and looking up each alley he passes. His manner is far more important than any facial makeup that he may wear, as most decoy operations will take place during the hours of darkness when facial features are not so clearly seen.

The officer chosen for the decoy role must have some talent for acting and he must be reasonably courageous to place him - or herself in the role of potential victim. The role can be any of several types: young girl walking alone, old man or old woman, shopper carrying grocery bag, bus driver, delivery boy, etc. Whatever the role, the officer must fit in, not only with his role but with his surroundings. The role of Caucasian girl walking alone would stand out as being illogical in a Black neighborhood, and an alcoholic bum would seem out of place in a conspicuously upper-class street. In the same way, a well-dressed businessman type would not normally be seen on skid row.

Sometimes the decoy can be an inanimate object. Auto theft gives a prime example. The police can place a particular type of car in a vulnerable location ripe for ripping off. If Cadillacs are in vogue among the car boosters that year, one can be parked on a dark street where it will make a tempting target to a cruising thief. This sort of decoy overlaps with a stakeout and really the difference is only one of hairsplitting definition rather than a substantial one.

There are a couple of problems peculiar to the police that will not obstruct the vigilante. The police must avoid a situation that would be interpreted by the courts as entrapment and they must concern themselves with the Miranda warning and giving the arrestee his rights. As the encounter is likely to be a violent one the police must also be careful to use only "reasonable and necessary force" to make the arrest. The vigilante need not pay much attention to these aspects of the action, as his actions are not subject to judicial review and curbstone justice usually involves the use of a lot of force.

The police also have a couple of advantages over the vigilante. They can, if necessary, call for help from the uniformed force on patrol. Reinforcements are only a radio call away. They can also obtain the cooperation of citizens more easily than can the vigilante, as flashing a badge will often be all that is necessary to commandeer a car, or premises from which to mount a stakeout.

Stakeouts usually involve fixed targets vulnerable to crime, such as banks, pharmacies, liquor stores. Where the police do not have to maintain a mobile operation, they can set up many points for surveillance of the subject premises and they will often substitute policemen for the store personnel. Additional police are hidden in a back room, behind furniture or curtains, and yet others may be stationed outside disguised as street vendors, telephone linemen, etc. More police might be parked in a car several hundred yards away, ready to come to the aid of the police on the spot or to take up pursuit if that becomes necessary.

The police can, if it becomes necessary, openly pursue their suspects with lights flashing and sirens screaming. They can call upon help from neighboring jurisdictions and continue the pursuit across a state line. This is a great advantage whose importance cannot be overrated.

The police usually have all the equipment that they need or want. With police budgets rising faster than those of most other government services the police have many handy items which the vigilante can only envy or try to improvise. The police assigned to a stakeout where shooting is expected will almost certainly be provided with bullet-resistant vests and of course they have their radios. Police radios are set to operate on a special band and some of them have built-in scramblers, for secrecy. Automatic weapons are in the arsenals of all but the tiniest police forces in the country.

All things considered, the police are well-trained and well-equipped to run decoy and stakeout operations against armed and dangerous felons. The vigilante, by contrast, has to struggle against several handicaps, not the least of which is being on the other side of the law.

When a vigilante decides to act as a decoy or to stake out premises against crime, he must first make several basic decisions:

a) The first one is whether to go with a team or to go it alone. In fiction, the hero usually goes it alone. Whether he is the mild-mannered little Death Wisher, walking his solitary path down the silent streets or through the somber roads in the park, or the ferocious and deadly Executioner type, the one-man army assaulting the headquarters of the Mafia with rockets, radar, and machine guns, he acts by himself. In real life the danger of doing so is extreme.

It is possible for a rugged, determined vigilante, skilled with weapons and adept in the martial arts, to survive many individual combats with muggers and robbers but such a person would probably not look much like the type who is routinely assaulted and mugged. It is difficult for a two hundred pound man to disguise himself as a girl or a little old grandmother.

While it is somewhat possible for a vigilante to act alone in certain circumstances if he takes prudent steps to limit the danger to himself, most of the time vigilantes choose to act in groups. One of the most important reasons for doing so, even though it is rarely discussed, is that of morale. People do tend to boost each other's morale in groups, while it takes a tremendous amount of emotional stamina to carry on alone.

b) The location of the decoy or stakeout is another factor to consider. Sometimes there is little choice. If liquor stores are being held up it does no good to stake out laundromats. For decoy operations there is more choice as it is mobile and the locale and route can be picked with care.

The obvious choice for many is a dark street or a lonely pathway in a park where muggers are known to hang out. There are other excellent possibilities, such as a crowded street in broad daylight, where many purse-snatchings occur. Daylight and crowds offer the prospect of hiding the vigilante team in plain sight, mingling with the crowds.

The location picked must satisfy several requirements, such as concealment for the team, easy access and escape routes, enough visibility for adequate surveillance, etc.

c) Another basic decision is who will be either the decoy or the front man in a stakeout. In a stakeout, usually the man behind the counter will be the legitimate proprietor or employee, who is part of the vigilante team anyway. In a decoy operation, the person selected to play the decoy must have strong nerves as well as some basic skill in acting. The decoy will not have to try to avoid acting like a cop, as he or she will not be a cop in the first place, but still it will take some talent to act a certain role. A favorite one is that of an old person, which involves a shabby overcoat, a stooped walk, and a slightly feeble and uncertain manner. A shopping or grocery bag is the customary prop for this role and for a vigilante it serves double duty in that it can contain a weapon ready for easy access.

In certain really dangerous situations, if the light is not too good, there can be a tear in the side of the grocery bag large enough to admit the hand and wrist of the person holding it. The hand inside the bag holds a pistol, ready to fire. This tactic eliminates the problem of drawing the weapon and it will give the person acting the role of decoy a greater sense of security.

In certain purse-snatching decoy jobs the decoy may choose to be armed but it should be obvious that the weapon not be carried in the purse.

If the decoy is part of a team the proper role is for him or her to offer no resistance to the criminal while they are in contact. The extreme danger to the decoy makes it imperative to assure the decoy's safety before any action is taken. The actual apprehension or sanction is applied during the felon's getaway. It can be as simple as the decoy drawing a pistol and shooting the felon in the back as soon as he turns to run, or it can consist of several members of the team blocking the felon's escape and taking appropriate action.

If the decoy is acting alone the appropriate moment to act is just before the felon strikes, as the danger of being wounded or incapacitated during the commission of the crime might preclude action after the fact. The difficulty of timing it properly is yet another reason for not acting alone.

The tactic to be followed in a decoy operation will vary with the situation and the purpose of the operation. The decoy can be static or mobile — a man waiting for a bus or a girl walking down a dark street. The role of a drunk ripe to be "rolled" can be played as a static part, which makes it easier on the other members of the team.

If the decoy is moving the other members of the team move along with him or her to provide surveillance and cover. They must be able to see without being seen. The cliche of several men in a car following a hundred yards behind is not really workable because it is too obvious. One good compromise is to have the decoy walk a limited path within sight of fixed positions taken by the other members of the team.

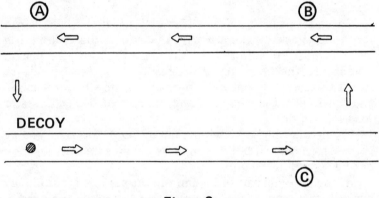

Figure 3

The decoy in Figure 3, in this case acting the role of a hooker, quite logically patrols her beat, a block along the "Strip" in this city. A, B and C are the other members of the team. A is located inside an all-night diner along the decoy's path and B is inside the first door in the lobby of a cheap walk-up. C is observing the scene from behind the window of a "knocking shop" hotel across the street from B. To make it look natural C has brought a female member of the team along but they are both alert and watching the decoy.

C is the control of this operation, as he has the best view from the second floor. He has the main walkie-talkie and will direct the operation with it.

Walkie-talkies can be helpful but they have their limitations too. They operate on the Citizens' Band and anyone can listen in. In this case the controller will use a very simple code to communicate with his people. One click of the transmit button every quarter hour will serve as a radio check, to confirm that the equipment is working properly. Two clicks will be the alert signal, signifying that he sees someone acting suspicously near the decoy. Three clicks will be the "move" signal, telling the people to move in and take whatever action had been previously decided. As it is cold weather the ones in the street are heavily dressed and carrying the radios in an overcoat pocket or clipped to the belt, with a "rubber duck" antenna for compactness.

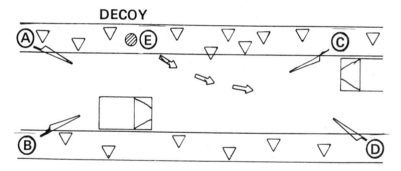

Figure 4

In Figure 4, the operation is conducted in broad daylight on a busy shopping street in an effort to stop purse snatchers. The decoy, a female carrying a purse very loosely on her shoulder in a way that is an open invitation to anyone having purse snatching in mind, walks along the sidewalk. The other members of the team, always at least four, walk along with her at several yards' distance, mingling with the crowds. They keep station with her as she walks along, crosses the street, etc.

The purse-snatcher, E, grabs the purse and, panicked by the screams of the woman acting as a decoy, runs out into the street so that he does not have to weave his way through the crowd. A, B, C, and D converge on him. Another way to deal with this is to have one or more of the team in a car on the street. The escaping E is in a good position to be run down in what can be made to appear as a motor accident.

If the action is confined to what can be done on foot because of no parking zones or some other reason, the team members intercepting the purse-snatcher can do a lot even in broad daylight and in front of many witnesses. The main reason that this will be possible is that the action takes place within a crowd. The purse-snatcher will not even be aware of the presence of the vigilantes until the attack materializes all around him. He can be tripped to get him down. Firearms will be of little use here because of the extreme danger to innocents in case of wild shots but a knife can be invaluable for inflicting a crippling or a lethal wound. The passers-by see a flurry of movement but then the members of the team move away from the purse-snatcher, some of them yelling: "This man's been hurt — call the police" as they blend into the crowd.

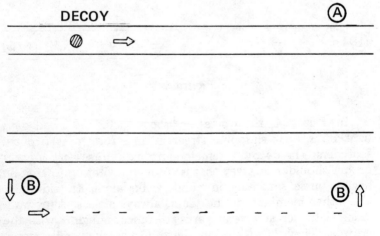

Figure 5

In the case of a decoy in a lonely area (Figure 5) it is not possible to blend in with a crowd, nor is it possible to adopt fixed positions for surveillance because the decoy must move. In that case the only tactic that will work is a "leapfrogging" operation, in which the watchers, after the decoy has passed and they have satisfied themselves that nobody is tracking the decoy at that moment, go to another position via a parallel street or an alley.

A big drawback to this type of operation is that it requires a lot of furtive movement by the watchers. This alone can attract the attention of the police. Another unpleasant prospect is that a member of the team, alone and uncovered while moving from one position to another, might fall victim to the type of criminal likely to be found in the area.

Stakeouts are very similar in tactics, in some ways. The main difference is that there is not a moving, animate target for the criminal. The criminal's target may be a car, or a cash register inside a liquor store, or the contents of a warehouse. Any people encountered along the way are only incidental. This does not reduce the possibility of a violent response by the criminal or the danger to the stakeout team.

One simple stakeout was in response to a series of attacks on parked cars in one neighborhood. Someone was breaking the windshields late at night or early in the morning.

Six men in three cars participated in the stakeout shown in Figure 6. Two men were in each car. One was in the front seat, the other sat in the back. This allowed the crew of each car to lie flat on the seat in order to be unseen by passing police patrols. The unfortunate sidelight on this affair is that although the area was regularly patrolled by the police they were unable to stop the vandalism, although they surely would have responded in a very negative way if they had discovered the men lying in wait for the vandal or vandals.

Car A was positioned to observe the goings-on along the street heading East and also to pursue with minimal delay anyone heading East, North, or South. Car B was in a blocking position with its crew ready to intercept anyone heading East or to start up and pursue anyone heading West. Car C was ready to chase anyone heading East, North, or South.

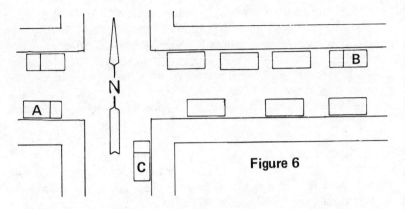

Figure 6

The plan was for the members of the crew nearest the observed incident to pile out and apprehend the vandals, and give chase on foot if necessary. The area was composed of "garden apartments" with wide lawns and passageways between the buildings, which made it possible for a suspect to flee through them to the next street.

The crews of the other cars would start engines and prepare to go around the block, if need be, to cut off the fleeing suspects. Another prospect was direct pursuit if they fled down the street directly. If the suspects had a car and tried to make their getaway with it, it was possible to block both ends of the block very quickly.

All members of the party were armed with clubs made out of bars of stainless steel wrapped with tape. A rifle was available in the back seat of one of the cars if the situation called for it.

The logistics were basically simple. As this took place in the cold season in a northern city, the team had to dress warmly. The car heaters could not be used because running the engines would have alerted everyone within hearing that there were people present. Early the previous evening one of the team collected .contributions from some of the other members, bought food, and made sandwiches to be consumed while on watch that night. Several members brought along thermos bottles of hot coffee for the vigil. In each car was an empty milk carton for the use of anyone who had to urinate.

As the author participated in this stakeout (as driver of car A; if anyone really wants to know) it is possible to give many details and provide some of the color that otherwise would be lacking.

The vigil was a cold and long one. The party made its way down to the cars singly between 10:00 and 11:00 P.M. Some of the equipment was already stowed in the cars so there was not very much to carry. Some of the team took benzedrine to keep them awake during the long night.

Every sixty to ninety minutes a police car passed and the team had to lay down to avoid being seen.

Well after midnight an old Chevy drove up and parked on the south side of the block being watched, several dozen yards in front of car A. There were a couple of figures in it barely visible in the light from the street lamps. They did not get out of the car. After a while it could be seen that they were locked in an embrace along the front seat and that the Chevy was rocking slightly.

This points up one of the everyday problems confronting the vigilante. Lacking police powers he cannot confront anyone who gets in his way and order them to move. He has to work his way around the problem by other means. In this case, the driver of car A, directly in line with the Chevy, decided that the courting couple might be there for an hour or more and that their continued presence might deter the vandal. He happened to have two powerful spotlights mounted on the roof of the car and he flicked these on for a brief burst, illuminating the couple in the Chevy. There was a scurrying in the front seat of the Chevy, a quick adjustment of clothing, and about a minute after the lights had come on the Chevy drove away. The risk from flashing the lights was minimal because it was so brief, and the party settled down to wait for the dawn or the vandals, whichever came first.

The vandals did not show up. Possibly they had seen the waiting men. Possibly they decided to move on to another neighborhood. Nobody was caught and no further incidents of broken windshields occurred.

In the case of staking out premises in danger of being robbed or vandalized, the vigilantes have several extreme advantages over the police and a few minor disadvantages. Usually the vigilante is the proprietor or an employee and is therefore already on the spot. He does not need to familiarize himself with the layout: he already knows it. If he is the proprietor he can have modifications made to help him in his task; for example, he can have a steel plate put in a chosen spot behind the counter or he can have the locks changed to suit his needs without consulting anyone else.

He has the advantage of secrecy. He is the person normally occupying the premises. There will be no strange men arriving with equipment at odd hours. He does not have to share his plan with anyone.

If he decides to get some help, such as that of other merchants who are in the same danger, he then is taking the risk of compromising secrecy only with other like-minded men, which is very little risk indeed. "Leaks" are unlikely.

A formal stakeout can be defined as a set-up where people who are not normally on the threatened premises occupy it to prevent or counteract criminals. That is what makes the difference between a stakeout and an attempt to resist intruders, as described earlier.

The situation described and illustrated in Figure 2 will be modified somewhat if the shopkeeper has some help. We can take another look at it in Figure 7.

In this case the storekeeper, C, has several helpers. Helper B, behind the counter, has a piece of steel plate built into the counter for protection and can duck down and open fire without hesitation, as the proprietor can duck behind the cash register H and the wall behind the stick-up man is block offering a solid backstop. If the robber takes the owner hostage and forces him through the door to the back, D can take him out as he comes through the doorway, as it is an easy shot from the closet and there are no obstructions to the field of fire. G is stationed in the alley to intercept the robber if he manages to get away. He can shoot him coming through the back door, if he comes that way, or he can go around and take him out as he tries to get to his car. As an alternative plan, G can disable the car while the robber is inside. If the robber is operating as part of a team, with a "wheelman"

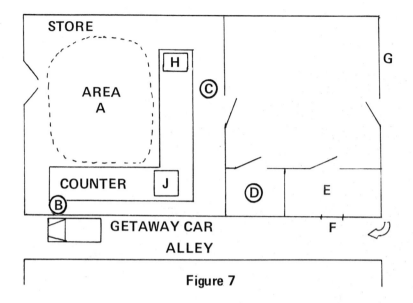

Figure 7

driving the getaway car, G's task will be to quietly dispose of the "wheelman" while the robbers are inside, before they have a chance to come out. In the actual incident upon which this description is based, the robber never made it to the car but the timing was close and it might happen differently next time.

The stack of goods, J, will still serve a useful purpose because it can't be taken for granted that the stakeout team will be in the exact positions shown in the diagram when the robbers come in. There is always a benefit in having an extra piece of cover or two.

The tactics involved in this stakeout are somewhat different from those described for Figure 2, as the owner of the shop has a lot of help with the problem. The importance that this has in minimizing the danger cannot be overemphasized.

In planning a stakeout one of the most important aspects, after providing for cover, is planning fields of fire. Several things must be considered when doing so: the safety of passers-by, crossfire, overlapping fields of fire, avoiding dead spots, and denying cover to the enemy.

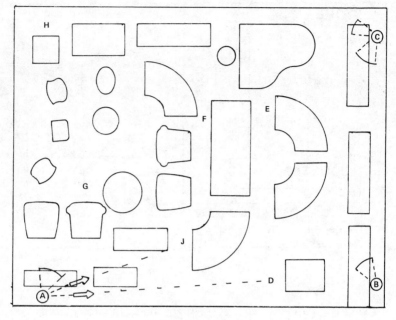

Figure 8

This is a composite of several situations to show the problems involved in planning fields of fire. No single situation is likely to have all of these problems but they are all possibilities which must be considered when planning a stakeout.

The locale is a furniture store in a neighborhood in which the merchants have been getting robbed regularly during the past several months. In this diagram there are three vigilantes taking the part of salesmen in the store. They are all armed and have pre-planned firing points from which to shoot when the robbery starts. The front of the store is at the left and there is a huge plate glass window taking up the whole front of the store. The street outside is crowded, which is normal in a shopping district. The other three sides are stone or block walls. There is no back room in this hypothetical case, there are also no closets or toilets.

The first vigilante, A has a position normally at the front of the store to greet customers as they enter. His firing point is behind the bookcase, which has a piece of sheet steel bolted to the back of it. He is limited in his arc of fire because he cannot fire toward the front of the store and he cannot fire directly at his two allies at the rear. B and C, working behind the counter at the rear of the store, are even more limited, as they cannot fire directly toward the front of the store either and must avoid shooting at A or at each other too. In addition, the various pieces of furniture in the store offer robbers varying degrees of cover or concealment.

Robber D, for example, is behind a refrigerator and this gives him both cover and concealment from both B and C. Only if he comes over to his left will he be open to some crossfire from C. Only A has a perfect shot at him, as the refrigerator will protect B from the bullets if he misses.

J is in a bad position, for he has taken cover behind a low sectional which is not really bullet resistant and he can be taken out by either B or C. He is exposed to crossfire and it is worthwhile here to look at precisely what crossfire means. Crossfire is gunfire coming from two different directions so that the person being fired upon cannot find cover from both. If he scurries around to one side of his cover to gain protection from one, the other has a clear shot at him.

Crossfire can be effective or ineffective at different ranges and arcs. There is an interrelationship between the cover available and the arcs of fire that determine whether crossfire will be effective in a particular case.

J is in a somewhat better position, for he is behind a sectional that puts him in a position where B and C cannot fire at him because it would mean firing toward the glass front of the store. Yet it is significant that he probably is not aware of this limitation. He will naturally assume that B and C, since they have guns, will fire at him. B also could not fire at D for the same reason, but D probably did not become aware of this until too late.

A's arc of free fire is only toward the side wall of the store but he can, if he frames his shot carefully, fire at both

D and at J. J is on a line from A to midpoint between B and C so A can fire at J if he is very careful.

F is behind a sofa and just within B's arc of fire. He is also in a position to take crossfire from A.

G is behind a club chair, which is not really bullet resistant but large enough to make him difficult to hit unless he exposes himself. He is out of B and C's arcs of fire but within A's. There is no crossfire here.

H has taken a position between a corner table and a desk. This is poor cover but because he is so far from B and C and right at the edges of their arcs of fire his position is not as bad as it seems. He is also far away from A, who has the best field of fire, and there is a lot of furniture in the way. With all these obstructions, A would perhaps have to expose himself more than usual to get a clear shot at H, or would have to change his position. This could be hazardous if the other robbers were still able to fire at this time.

The tactical positions of A, B, and C also need to be examined. They are all behind cover, which means protected positions, and are not exposed to crossfire, with the possible exception of A. He might be vulnerable to fire from a gang member left outside the store as a lookout or a "wheelman", and firing in at him through the window. All three vigilantes, then, are in easily defensible positions and have arranged things so that the robbers are caught between them.

Another aspect of this situation worth noting is the short ranges involved. An idea of the scale can be gotten from the size of the furniture shown: its scale as it appears in this book is roughly 1/8" = 1 foot. The maximum distance between antagonists is the range between B and H, which is about thirty feet. Shootouts, particularly those which take place indoors, take place at very close ranges.

There are several other problems associated with running a stakeout. One is what to do with the bodies and the blood. Most of the time the shooting will occur in an urban setting and there is absolutely no way to conceal the events from the police. In fact, doing so would be a felony and getting caught at it would be very undesireable.

Usually the explanation is very simple. The robbers attempted to rob the store and got shot for their troubles. The problems begin when there is more than one participant on the shopkeeper's side. Explaining away one other person is not too difficult — a close friend who happened to drop in as the robbery was in progress or just before. His just knowing that there was a shotgun in the back room is plausible. If there is more than one ally, however, it becomes hard to believe that a whole bunch of close friends "just happened" to be on the scene at the right moment and that they all "just happened" to be armed. If there are strict gun control laws in that locale the situation becomes even more difficult. The police are not going to react favorably to the evidence of a major gun battle with vigilantes as participants no matter what the outcome.

Another problem, which is even more serious, is that of innocent people being caught in the shootout and injured or killed. This is not a problem if they are shot by robbers, it happens all the time. If they have caught a bullet fired by the vigilantes it opens up the unpleasant prospect of a Murder One charge.

The worst possible case, from the practical side and from the moral point of view, is that of the shopkeeper who kills in self-defense with an unregistered gun in a locale which has both strict gun laws and an ineffective police force. One such is New York City, which has a police force that has had many corruption scandals, which has a crime rate that is either the top in the nation or close to it, and which has the strictest gun laws in the nation. They are so strict that even air guns are outlawed.

In such a case, there is usually a technicality in the law that says that any homicide committed during the commission of another felony is automatically Murder One. The intent is to facilitate prosecution of a robber or mugger who kills his victim, even inadvertently. In practice, it means that someone using an unregistered gun in self-defense, if he kills his assailant, will face a charge of Murder One if owning an unregistered gun is a felony.

This is not just an interesting anomaly in the law because several people have been prosecuted for exactly this. One seventy year old man, killing an armed intruder with an unregistered .38 caliber pistol, was so charged by a frustrated police department that had no one else to prosecute. You cannot prosecute a dead man, so they took second best and prosecuted the survivor.

In another notorious case, a young lady fought off a rapist with a switchblade, which falls under New York's concealed weapons law. She was charged, but not with murder, as the assailant survived. The case went to trial, much to the shame of the police and the District Attorney, but the jury acquitted her, having their own wives and daughters to worry about.

All of these cases point up the risks involved in trying to do the police's job for them. The risks are real and they are many, and only the most careful planning will minimize them.

In decoy operations, the risks from the law are minimal because the vigilantes in principle walk away from the scene, leaving the police to sort out what happened. In a stakeout the vigilantes have to remain and make the explanations.

Some ways which have been used to reduce the risks are:

A) Hiding the body and the evidence of the action. This is possible only if the locale is isolated (a warehouse district after business hours) and there are no outside witnesses.

B) Fudging the evidence. The vigilantes can, if time permits, disappear before the arrival of the police, and the shopkeeper can claim that there was a shootout, that he did shoot a couple of the bandits, that there were a lot of wild shots and that some of the bandits got away. This can be a very thin story but it has been known to work.

C) Taking the action elsewhere. Sometimes no shots are fired: the very appearance of armed and determined men cause the robbers to surrender. Sometimes the survivors will surrender after one of their number is killed. This reduces the mess that has to be explained away. The survivors can be transported elsewhere for disposal.

D) Leaving immediately. This is only possible in the

most unlikely case: that the action takes place on someone else's property without their knowledge or presence. It is very hard to arrange and when it is the tactics governing decoys rather than stakeouts will apply.

Yet another aspect to consider is the appropriate response to the felon. In some cases the issue is forced: if there is armed resistance the felon will be killed on the spot. In some types of situations this will not occur and the offense is not even a major one. Then some fine judgment is required. The actions which vigilantes have taken in the past are covered in the chapter on sanctions but a further explanation of some of the pros and cons is worthwhile.

Prevention is a prime object of a vigilante action. The crime is stopped right there and that alone justifies action in most cases.

Deterrence is another prime reason but the effectiveness is harder to judge. Of course, if a whole series of muggers are found shot to death the lesson will sink in and even the most crime-ridden community will begin to show an improvement.

In an effort to enhance the deterrent effect, some vigilantes are tempted to leave a "calling card" in some operations. This might be the fictional marksman's medal or something radically different but still symbolic, such as a noose. Such a dramatic device does have the effect of sensationalizing the event and of making it more newsworthy, thereby guaranteeing that the word will be spread. It also serves as a direct affront to the police, who will then make an effort to catch the vigilantes as intense as that to catch the original criminals. That raises the level of risk for any future operation.

One effect of disposing of the felon is that of removing what might be a troublesome witness. The felon might even be a psychopath who might set out on getting revenge. This makes him doubly dangerous and thereby a prime candidate for immediate execution.

One consequence of police interest in the case has yet to be considered. In certain instances the police may resort to decoys of their own to trap the vigilantes, or they may stake out the area of operation. The first tactic is not a very great danger, as the vigilante does not act until the felon actually strikes but the police stakeout is a very real danger. The peril is made worse because the vigilante, if confronted by the police, cannot shoot his way out of the situation because he is basically on the side of law and order.

Several other types of stakeouts have to be considered. These are the stakeouts with the prospect of pursuit, the remote stakeout, and the stakeout on the subway. The case of the subway stakeout is perhaps the most interesting, so we will look at it first.

The group presently grabbing the headlines, the "Red Berets", patrols the New York subways in a distinctive uniform consisting of a white tee-shirt and a red beret. Their action cannot really be considered a stakeout because they patrol openly. They get a lot of publicity, which for various reasons is undesireable for a vigilante, and their presence can act as a deterrent to subway toughs. However, more effective action can be taken by vigilantes who patrol incognito rather than in a conspicuous outfit. Every year several bodies are found on the subway in circumstances which do not immediately suggest robbery or rape as the motive. Some of these are due to vigilantes carrying out their swift and silent vigils, emerging from the shadows only momentarily and then vanishing again into the city's underground. Some of them may be policemen putting in some unpaid overtime in an effort to make a meaningful impact on the city's crime problem. Some are otherwise ordinary citizens who go to work during the day, raise families, and pay taxes like everybody else.

The subway stakeout is perhaps the easiest of all to accomplish. The vigilante has only to ride the subway, preferably late at night, the time of low traffic and peak crime. Pretending to doze, sitting back upon the seat with the hands in the pockets of the overcoat, is the favorite way. The task is not physically exhausting, although it requires strong nerves. The noise of the train will hide the sounds of shots and the next station will provide an easy escape.

People who do not ride the subway regularly may not be aware that those who do mind their own business, even if they are the subway police. A passenger seen slumped over in his seat is assumed to be dozing and not to be disturbed. This makes disposal of the body very easy for the vigilante. Even if the next station along the line is crowded, propping the deceased mugger up on a seat, pulling his hat down over his face, and calmly walking out will usually assure that the formerly ferocious felon will ride to the end of the line.

Since May, 1980, the number of people riding the New York subway system has been declining, according to figures published in the New York Times. The reason is obvious: subway crime. The biggest subway system in the world has the worst crime problem in the world. One of the sidelights of the worsening situation is the effort by vigilantes to cope with that problem.

The stakeout with the prospect of pursuit can be dealt with very quickly. Basically, only the established police have the means to carry out a pursuit. The vigilante will most likely attract the unfavorable attention of the police if he tries to pursue a fleeing felon. Figure 6 showed a situation where a pursuit was likely, but it was most likely to be done on foot and over a very short distance. If the criminal had had to be chased for more than a block the effort would have had to be abandoned, as there was a crowded area nearby and constant police patrols. There was a slight chance that the vandal would try to get away in a car, but to forestall this the ends of the street could be immediately blocked.

In other situations, every effort is usually made to ensure that all exists are closed off, or at least can be closed immediately. In the store stakeout, Figure 7, the suspect's car is disabled before he can make his getaway.

In effect, the only rational course for the vigilante is to stop the escape right at the outset, either by overwhelming firepower or by disabling or blocking the suspect's means of escape. Prolonged pursuit is not feasible.

Of course, the distinction must be made between hot pursuit and the long pursuit that vigilantes of the past used. Hot pursuit, with shots fired and cars screaming around corners, is what is unfeasible today. The long pursuit, tracking a wanted person over many miles and running him down far from home, is still just as workable as it was in the old days. All that it requires is time, money, and luck.

The remote stakeout is possibly the most complicated type that is attempted by vigilantes, and to illustrate this an example will be given that was mentioned in passing earlier, that of a stakeout that began on the premises and ended across the road.

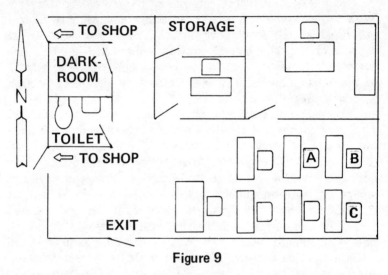

Figure 9

There were three participants in this action, one of the longest and most inconclusive actions in the author's knowledge. The foreman and two trusted employees of a shop in a city in the Western United States decided to do something about an epidemic of sabotage that was causing a lot of problems. There had been much speculation as to who was the culprit and the only thing that seemed clear was that the saboteur had to be someone who either worked there or had worked there recently, as the damage done indicated some knowledge of the operation. It was not the common rock-through-the-window type of damage but specialized disabling of the equipment.

They decided to return after their shift ended and to remain inside on watch through at least half the night, until the likely bedtime of most people or later. What happened illustrates several of the problems that beset the vigilante.

At first, after driving away, they returned and came back in through a back door to the shop that they had left open for this purpose. After quickly searching the shop to make sure that nobody else had entered through this convenient way, they took up positions in the office, behind the rearmost desks. They had prepared for their vigil by bringing sandwiches, coffee, pistols, and a can of Mace. It was anticipated that the culprit would not be armed, in which case the physical force of three men and perhaps a shot of Mace would handle the situation. There was always the possibility that armed resistance would be offered, hence the pistols. At the outset, there was not a clear idea what to do with the culprit if he were caught. It was a choice of either giving him a beating or turning him over to the police. This potential weakness in the plans never caused any problem, for the suspect never turned up.

It was necessary to sit in darkness for many hours, talking only in low tones and carefully shielding the light of the occasional cigarette. One aspect of keeping a vigil that is never told in fiction is the many false alarms. At night, when on the alert for any strange noise or occurrence, it is easy to hear every creak and groan that a building makes, and to misinterpret every wind noise.

The basic plan was simple and flexible. It was to approach and confront the intruder as soon as possible after he had made his illegal entry into the building. The light switches were near the doorways into the shop, allowing the vigilantes to flood the premises with light at the appropriate moment while remaining in the dark themselves.

One possibility that had been considered was that the saboteur might be the owner himself, as his reputation in business was not the best and he was not above doing damage to collect on the insurance.

Occasionally during the vigils the watchers took places inside the shop, trying to find positions that allowed them some comfort yet gave them the best concealment and the best view of the possible sites of entry and of sabotage. Some thought was also given to surrounding the intruder if he ever showed up, and blocking his escape.

Another feature of staking out that came to light during this affair was the drain of the physical stamina of the participants, who had to put in a long day's work five days a week and then take up the watch. The effort this demanded was so severe that they were able to mount the stakeout only three days out of each week, on the average. The foreman, who lived nearby, would occasionally drive by for a spot check at other times, when he had the opportunity, but it was not possible to give the premises one hundred percent coverage. There were many gaps in the guard and incidents of sabotage continued to happen.

On one occasion there occured an incident which demonstrated some of the difficulties vigilantes face, not having police powers. One of the participants, on his way to pick up another at his home where he was fixing coffee and sandwiches, goodnaturedly stopped to pick up a hitch-hiker, not realizing that the hitch-hiker was very drunk and wanted only to go to sleep in the car. After a while, when the drunk refused to either state where he wanted to go or to get out of the car, the driver realized that he had a serious problem on his hands. He picked up the other man, and they discussed the best way of solving this latest kink in their plans. One suggestion considered was to drive down to the nearby rail yards, a very quiet place at this time of night, and force the drunk out at gunpoint. The prospect of having probably to shoot him was unpleasant, for it is not a capital crime to be drunk. They finally decided to drive to a nearby police station to have the police remove the drunk from the car. The drunk spent the night in jail, not realizing that he had come reasonably close to losing his wasted life that night. The vigilantes drove on to rejoin the foreman and to tell him what had happened. The foreman found the account so improbable and unbelieveable that to this day he thinks that it was just a fantasy or a joke. The vigil continued.

After several weeks of trying to catch the vandal the vigilantes decided to change their tactics. They felt that perhaps the vandal might be aware that they were staking out the building, as one of the suspects was an ex-employee who lived across the street and down the block. Although the vigilantes were careful to park their cars in the parking lot of the shopping center across the main road, and to take a roundabout route to the back of the building, there was still this possibility. What made it more likely was the possibility that the vandal knew their cars, having seen them in the parking lot of the shop during working hours, and scouted the area for any familiar cars before making his entry.

They therefore decided to try a remote stakeout from the parking lot of the shopping center, never approaching the building and choosing a position from which although they could not see all of the entrances, they could watch the approaches to the building. They also kept on the alert for any familiar cars cruising the area, as there was even a chance of the vandal parking in the parking lot while he went over to do his damage.

The shop was located on Evan Lane, around the corner from Redman Road and behind a gas station. Next to the gas station was a small shopping center with a laundry, pizza parlor, and a convenience market. The basic layout is shown in Figure 10 on the next page.

There were three entrances to the shop, with entrance number 1 right into the back building, C. Right next to entrance number 1 was a loading dock and gate, which normally was kept securely locked. Entrance number 2 was into the office, A, and the third entrance led directly into the back building but on the South side, in a corner that could not be seen either from the street or from the parking lot in the shopping center across Redman Road.

Part B of the main building was a shop area but had no entries directly from the outside. Anyone wanting to get into that part would have to come in from the office or the back building. All three doors were normally kept locked at night but a section of corrugated iron wall in the back building was loose and offered an entry to anyone who knew about it.

Across Evan Lane were detached houses. In one of them lived a former employee who was a potential suspect. The open areas between the buildings were used for parking during

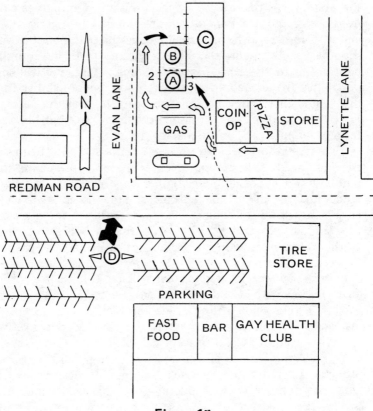

Figure 10

the day. The little shopping center had a lot of traffic, both during the day and at night, which complicated the surveillance problem, as we shall see.

In the shopping center on the South side of Redman Road there were parking areas from which the watch was kept. Nearest to the selected area were a fast food restaurant, a bar, and a health club frequented by homosexuals, which indirectly led to complications. The tire store closed at six.

Observation was kept from the area marked D, the exact place being determined by the availability of parking among the other cars. Whatever the position chosen, though, it was impossible to see all of the entries to the building being watched. The number 3 entry was masked by the gas station building. Entry 2 was in plain sight and though entry 1 was not, anyone turning off to go to it could be seen.

To make the task harder, much of the traffic into and from the little shopping center was on foot. The people living around the corner from it on Evan Lane often went there to do their laundry or to buy a container of milk or a pizza. Many of them took a short cut through the open area between the gas station and the buildings being watched. The watchers had to be aware of everyone who went into that area and to keep an eye out to see if they emerged from the other side within a few seconds or not. The street lighting was typical city street lighting, which illuminated the sidewalks well but left deep shadows between the buildings off the street. The people walking through the space between the buildings could not be clearly seen all the way through. The route is shown by the white arrows. When several people went through at the same time from both directions it became a problem of frantically counting heads and hoping that nobody had been missed.

With the conditions being what they were, a pair of 7X50 "night glasses" brought by one of the vigilantes were of only marginal help, and there were a number of false alarms. When this happened the vigilantes moved out according to plan. Usually two cars were used, with the watchers clustering together in one for the surveillance. The second car would be parked right next to it, and when the time came to move out the driver of the second car would jump out and get into it. Car 1, with two men in it, would go across Redman Road and through the space between the coin-op laundry and the gas station, shown by the dotted line and black arrow, and stop with the headlights on the door to building C. The occupants would get out and go into the building to search for and possibly confront any intruders.

The second car would go right up Evan Lane to stop with the headlights illuminating the dark corner where entrance number 1 was located, but far back enough so that the front door to the office could be seen. The driver stayed with the car, as his function was to block escape by anyone trying to get out of either door. Any intruder would, therefore, be caught between the advancing party from car 1 and the stopper from car 2.

Inside the buildings the search procedure was simple and sound, consisting basically of a leapfrogging operation, with one member staying behind cover and "covering" the other as he went to the next piece of cover or place to be searched. During the first false alarm, however, the members all went in together, not realizing that in doing so they left the back door open, so to speak, through which anyone could have escaped.

Parking across Redman Road was no problem, as the vigilantes deliberately chose a position away from the businesses so that they would not be taken for stickup men casing the place. This pointed up one of the limitations that plague vigilantes. If the police had run the stakeout they would not have had to worry about this problem. Another problem came about because of the flocking of homosexuals to the health club. One night a car with three men in it started circling around the three vigilantes in the parking lot. The vigilantes quickly realized that the occupants of the other car were not detectives, as policemen would have stopped and confronted them. They became aware that they were being "cruised" by three men who were going to or coming out of the health club. Not being policemen, the vigilantes could not stop the occupants of the other car and order them to clear the area.

This was another example of the problems that vigilantes face, having no official powers. Civilians often get in the way of operations and it is difficult to work around them at times. The vigilantes cannot set up roadblocks, or flash badges, or request cooperation. They have to work their way around the problem by other means.

In this case it was decided to bluff. It was obvious that the men in the other car were considering the possibility that the watchers might be police in plain clothes, so it was decided to act in a way that suggested that they were. The next time the car passed in front, the vigilante next to the driver raised his binoculars and ostentatiously scanned the members of the other party. Then the driver started his engine, turned on his lights, and started after them. It was a bluff, but it worked. The other car accelerated sharply and turned down the alley behind the tire store. As the vigilante car made the turn into the alley the occupants could see the other car speeding away far ahead of them, and then turn a corner and disappear for good. The incident offered a comic relief to the whole situation, but it did distract attention from the main task. The vigilantes made their way back to their parking space for the night and resumed their observation of the buildings.

This operation brought out other problems that vigilantes have to face. The most obvious is the need for patience and good judgment. Often the amount of time spent on a stake-out or decoy operation is great and the rewards are few. A stakeout can absorb many man-hours with no results. It is easy to get discouraged and to give up. What is not so obvious is that it is easy to go the other way too and to get trigger-happy. In this operation there were times during the false alarms when it would have been easy to shoot first and to ask questions later. A man fumbling by a dark doorway might be an intruder or just a drunk relieving himself in the first dark corner he could find. It is easy to imagine a person walking away from a building as having just come out of it, if one is overimaginative.

Another hazard is the official police. While it is not illegal for three men to spend most of the night sitting in a car in a public place, questioning by a passing police patrol was a danger to be avoided by trying to be inconspicuous, crouching down whenever a police car was seen.

31. On The Fringe:
Working With The Police

Participating in an "Operation Blockwatch" or a similar operation under the auspices of the official police is definitely not within our definition of vigilantism but some people do it and there is something to be gained from it, even for vigilantes.

There are several kinds of programs being tried in various parts of the country, with varying degrees of success. In New York, a number of "Blockwatch" type programs are run from time to time. This involves volunteers watching for suspicious activities on each block and calling the police if they see anything.

In Port Hueneme, California, a "Block Parent" program was started as a countermeasure against child molesters. Volunteers were screened and those deemed suitable were appointed to be "Block Parents". They would display a poster in their windows whenever they were home, so that passing children would know that this was a place where they would find help if needed. The "Block Parents" were told to report any incidents to the police.

A "Truckers' Alert" system was used in New York and in New Jersey, using radios installed in trucks. What it was, basically, was a way of broadcasting the description of a stolen rig so that thousands of truckers in the area would be looking out for it.

In Monterey Park, California, a Peoples' Anti-Crime Effort, PACE for short, was used to disseminate information to citizens who offered to help the police. The police handed out leaflets on precautions to take against burglars and other types of criminals. The emphasis was on crime prevention through enhanced security.

In all of these cases the police were emphatically telling the citizens involved that they were not to take any action on their own but were to call the police upon seeing any suspicious activity. Such an injunction is typical of the police's disapproval of citizens' doing anything to directly help themselves, but sometimes such an operation can be exploited by vigilantes for their own purposes.

In all cases the vigilantes must operate in areas where they are normally on the spot. For example, it would be difficult for vigilantes to park near a schoolyard to watch for child molesters. Most likely someone would report them to the police as being suspicious characters and a police car would soon pull up behind them. On the other hand, someone living on a street next to a school is in an excellent position to watch and to have other people in the house with him to help. A vigil can be maintained without anyone else becoming curious or even being aware that anything at all is going on. Naturally, the vigilantes need not actively join in the officially-sponsored effort to do this. Information as to the nature of the threat and the police activities to combat it can be obtained from a neighbor or a member of the family who has joined, gotten a membership card, and attended the meetings.

The central problem with any sort of "Blockwatch" or "Block Parent" program for the vigilante is the same as with a stakeout — the amount of time it consumes. Thousands of man-hours can pass without a single reward.

On the other hand, listening in on the radio when a "Truckers' Alert" type program is in effect can be more rewarding, if one is normally driving around in the area and would actually be in a position to do something positive. A vigilante who spots a stolen rig being driven off to a hideout will not call the police, of course. He will either take immediate action or follow the rig to get information as to where it is being taken for trans-shipment and then relay that information to other members of his group, who will then decide on the appropriate action.

Sometimes the vigilante has a stroke of luck. It can

happen, for example, that he sees his neighbor's house being burgled one day. This offers an excellent opportunity for action if he can show good judgment and be discreet about it. In a hypothetical example, he watches, notes down the license number of the burglar's truck, and waits until the burglar is finished and moves out. Meanwhile, he has telephoned to another vigilante to come join him, parking on the next street and coming in through the backyard. When the burglar gets into his truck, the vigilantes do not confront and John Wayne him on the spot. That would cause a police investigation right on their doorstep. Instead they follow him to his home or to where he disposes of the stolen goods. If the burglar goes home they can interrogate him before disposing of him. If he goes to a "fence" they can note the location and decide whether the appropriate action is best taken now or later. Whenever action is taken, an anonymous phone call to the police can be made to ensure that the stolen property will be returned to its owner. The burglar and the fence can be disposed of in the usual manner.

In the case of the classical child molester the pattern is even simpler. It requires two people. A child molester will flee if an adult approaches, particularly if the adult seems to know the child. A woman can serve in this role. When the molester is seen trying to entice the child into his car, the adult approaches on foot, talking to the child but showing no suspicion that anything is wrong. As the molester drives away, another vigilante follows him in his car. Killing the degenerate on the spot would only make an ugly scene and compromise the whole operation. Following him home is more discreet and offers more time to plan his disposal. It must be emphasized that knowing the child by name is likely only if the vigilantes are people who live in the neighborhood and not strangers from miles away.

The successful pattern is that vigilantes patrol their own neighborhoods but do the executions miles away.

Sometimes this is not possible. Some years ago, when urban riots were common, some residents of a small apartment house got together to plan for defense if the riots should reach the area. All had guns, and they planned for the defense of their homes if the rioters actually came onto their street. It was recognized that if the rioters got that far the police would have been pretty well overwhelmed and that probably there would be no searching investigation afterward into the subtleties of "self-defense". The plan was simple: Man the windows and shoot on sight. As the apartment house was the tallest building on the block the height would give a good overall view and a field of fire behind any available cover on the street, such as brick walls, cars, etc.

32. Impersonating Policemen

Impersonating policemen is a felony. It can also be very unsuccessful. There are, nevertheless, situations in which vigilantes find it rewarding to impersonate officers of the law.

One of these, obtaining information from a witness to or victim of a crime, has already been covered.

Another is in arresting and interrogating suspects. A quiet way to carry out a "snatch" is to persuade the suspect to come willingly. Many criminals have an open contempt for the police, feeling that they are not vulnerable to prosecution. This is particularly true of major career criminals, who feel that they have covered their tracks so well that the police will never be able to build a case against them. Some street criminals also feel this way, as the Miranda Decision has given them a measure of protection and current police practice is such that they sometimes are out on bail before the policeman finishes writing his report.

Flashing a badge is more effective in persuading a suspect to come quietly than saying "vigilante", which may not be believed and if it is, will result in only the most determined resistance.

Another situation in which claiming to be the police is of value is in a stakeout. For example, in a store stakeout against stick-ups, yelling "Freeze, police" is more likely to obtain the surrender of the stick-up artist than anything else. The criminals have a certain confidence in the police, in that they feel assured that they will not be mistreated.

It can be very convenient for the vigilante to persuade the criminal to surrender without a shot. Apart from avoiding the personal danger which a shootout carries with it, a surrender permits the vigilantes to keep their low profiles, transporting the criminals elsewhere for disposal.

The vigilante who decides to impersonate the police in such a situation need not concern himself with a badge. A stickup man looking down the barrel of a gun will not worry about the display of a badge or the lack thereof. What does count is the decisive and forceful manner that the police are in the habit of displaying. Adding to the color is the use of obscenities in the best police tradition. "Asshole" is a favorite term of endearment used by the police towards those who provide them with their livelihoods. Many of those who would be out of a job if it were not for criminals use even more colorful and imaginative terms, depending on local traditions.

What is as important as a forceful manner is handcuffs, which aid in restraining a prisoner for transportation. For various reasons it may be desireable to have the prisoner arrive at the destination alive. He will be easier to handle without deadly force if he is restrained in a manner that suggests police instead of vigilante. He will be perhaps more cooperative in interrogation if he still believes that he is dealing with the police, and may "talk" more than would be expected, as he will probably be sophisiticated enough to know that information obtained under any but the conditions laid out in recent court decisions cannot be used against him in court. Therefore, fostering the belief that he is in the hands of the police as long as possible is a definite aid to the vigilantes.

33. The Policeman-Vigilante

In the earlier years of this century it was accepted practice for the police to administer a sort of primitive justice right on the street. Summary punishments were often meted out for minor offenses and as a warning to more serious criminals, because "curbstone justice" was a tradition, just as was "frontier justice".

Today, as everyone knows, the situation is entirely different and the law no longer bends to allow the individual policeman on his beat to administer summary justice as he sees fit. Some view this as progress: some do not. The fact is that any policeman who administers curbstone justice today does so at the risk of his job and his personal freedom, for he may be dismissed and even prosecuted if he is caught at it.

With all that, some policemen still do administer their own version of justice. By far, most do so out of a sense of outrage against the criminal rather than any personal quirk of sadism. Sadistic cops are few and far between, and they are screened out as soon as possible because that sort of personality is not an asset to any police department.

The policeman who decides to be his own vigilante has an easier time of it than a civilian, for he wears the gun and the badge and can carry them openly. When an incident occurs, his version of it goes into the report, and often his is the only version that will be accepted. He comes into contact with criminals as a part of his job. He investigates and asks questions, develops information and follows it up. He can call upon the resources of his entire department in some instances.

For some, becoming a vigilante is as easy as squeezing the trigger when confronting a criminal. An armed criminal who decides to surrender can easily be shot anyway, with the official report stating that he resisted arrest. If there are no witnesses there is no problem at all.

The unarmed criminal is disposed of with a device called the "alibi gun" or "alibi knife", which is a small untraceable weapon that the officer carries upon his person for just this purpose: planting on the body of someone he has shot. Many policemen carry a second, smaller gun as a "backup" weapon. This is so they are not totally unarmed if they lose their service pistol or it is taken from them. If the gun is a fairly new, expensive one purchased under their own name, it can be taken at face value. If it is an old, nondescript weapon that was obtained by informal purchase from a stranger or confiscated from a criminal on the street it may well be an alibi gun. The same applies to a knife, which is far from being the customary police weapon.

Police have easy access to confiscated weapons. It is not necessary to make one disappear from the police property room, with all the fuss and scandal that this can cause. Many people stopped and searched by the police do carry something or other that can be carried as a weapon, and this can be summarily confiscated by the officer and the suspect dismissed with a warning. The suspect will not be clamoring to get his property back, inasmuch as it might be stolen and in any event he is glad to be released with no further ado. The conscientious collector can build up quite a stockpile by methods such as these. Some do.

In a milder vein, some policemen still use physical force to intimidate suspects. This practice varies with the locale and in some parts of the country it is customary for this to happen without prosecutions against the officer. In some cases a prosecution would be unlikely, as in the case of a burglar who is beaten up instead of arrested, and could not report the incident without compromising himself.

In other cases, there are what only can be called provoked shootouts, where a policeman confronts a suspect whom he knows to be armed in such a way that the suspect goes for his gun, giving the officer the "right" to shoot him down. Closely allied to this is the practice of "shooting first and asking questions later", for some a standard procedure in case of a holdup call. The police shoot the felon regardless of the circumstances, secure in the knowledge that they can establish legal justification. Taking no prisoners does save the officer time in court and the state the expense of a trial.

Another way in which police save the taxpayer the cost of a trial is by not being unduly hurried in summoning medical help for a seriously wounded suspect. Sometimes this is not possible but the ambulance can, with the cooperation of the driver, be delayed on the way to the hospital. There is a rumor that John Dillinger was disposed of this way.

Finally, there are the notorious but mysterious "death squads", bands of policemen who take criminals out to a convenient place and execute them with little fuss and fanfare. In this country it is sporadic rather than systematic, but in other countries it is almost the norm. In Brazil, the activities of the police death squads has become a scandal but mainly because they have a political coloration, which does not quite fit into our definition of vigilantism.

Death squads have all of the advantages. They can "arrest" their candidates for exterminating with no difficulty because they are, after all, the police. They are immune from interference from other policemen because of what is known as the "code". They have the specialized knowledge that makes it easy for them to cover their tracks. Finally, if it is the members of the death squad who have the responsibility for the investigation if the body is ultimately discovered, they can sidetrack the inquiry and interpret the case as another "gangland" killing.

34. The Dirty White Collar

White collar crime is a special case and thereby requires special handling. A crooked company cannot be punished in the same way as can a crooked individual. Complicating the problem is the fact that responsibility may be spread among several individuals who are in leading positions in a company pursueing unethical practices. It would be a mistake to say that it is all because of "the system", however. If everybody is guilty then nobody is guilty and nothing can be done.

The problem is separating the guilty from the innocent. Generally it is the executives who are the guilty ones, for they make the decisions and reap most of the benefits. The "working stiffs" who punch a time clock basically are only following orders and may not even know what is going on The truck driver who is ordered to deliver a cargo to a certain address cannot know if the television sets he is carrying are stolen. The body shop man who welds a new front end on a car does not necessarily know if the assembly he is using was from a stolen car or a salvaged one. The shoe clerk sells a pair of shoes from a hijacked cargo in the same way as he sells a pair that was legally procured.

The actions taken by vigilantes against a criminal company fit into two categories: actions against the company itself and actions against individuals within it. In any event the action will be something less severe than execution, as white collar crime is a crime against property and calls for retaliation in kind. The actions against the company are designed to hit where it hurts: in the profits, and the actions against certain selected individuals within it are for the purpose of disrupting their lives; in one word, harassment.

To do a maximum job of harassment against a company

it is necessary to have a certain amount of "inside information" about the company. For example, a vigilante wanting to send telegrams to the employees telling them not to report for work a certain day must have a list of employees and their addresses. Unless the vigilante is an employee or he knows someone who is, the method that will work best is trashing.

Using harassment against an individual is particularly attractive to the vigilante because it involves no personal contact and little risk. The security precautions needed for harassment are those that the vigilante normally takes anyway and the methods are easy to apply. A few highlights will illustrate the possibilities:

The individual can wind up with his light, water, and gas turned off. A few phone calls will do it.

His mail can be diverted by means of a change of address card to the Post Office. This tactic has been used very successfully.

His peace and quiet can be disturbed by people delivering liquor, pizzas, and other take-out items at all hours.

He can be kept busy answering telephone calls made in reply to ads placed in his name in the local newspaper.

His mailbox can be stuffed to overflowing by magazines ordered for him. His name can be put on the membership lists of many book clubs.

Various types of merchandise can be ordered in his name from companies doing business by mail or phone.

Gifts can be ordered by phone for people he does not even know, and billed to his telephone.

His house can be advertised for sale. People will be ringing his bell for days.

Posters can magically appear in every bar in town advertising an "open house" at his address in honor of the Fourth of July, Veterans' Day, New Year's, etc.

False official papers can be filed on his behalf, such as Form 1040 to the IRS.

A complete treatment of the subject of harassment is available in the books of that title put out by Desert Publications.

35. Delivering Warnings

In many situations vigilantes have considered a warning to be the appropriate action. If the subject heeded the warning it was not necessary to take more drastic measures. Often the vigilantes' reputation was enough to persuade the subject to cooperate.

Many times the warning was in the form of a cryptic sign or symbol, or a sequence of letters or numbers. The message was not usually spelled out, but was generally understood to be either "cease and desist" or "be out of town by sundown."

Today warnings have to be more explicit than that. There are so many strange communications being delivered that a vigilante's warning is likely to be mistaken for a publicity stunt, a crank call or note, or something delivered to the wrong address.

The vigilante who decides to deliver a warning in addition to, or instead of, drastic action is operating under a handicap. His letter may be thrown away without being taken seriously. In one case years ago, a vigilante sent a note to a crooked garage operator and found to his dismay that absolutely nothing resulted from the note. The garage owner did not even call the police.

The vigilante who wants to be believed and taken seriously enough for his warning to have an effect will usually find, unless there has been a lot of vigilante action in his locale, that he has to give the subject a taste of what can happen in order to gain his attention. Hypothetically, let us return to that garage owner who was ripping off people who brought their cars in for repairs.

If the vigilante first sent him a good many magazine subscriptions and waited for them to arrive, he would have been able to send the garage operator a note something like this:

"You've been ripping off people with your gyps long enough. We, the vigilantes, are going to do something about it but first we're going to give you one last chance to straighten up and fly right. You know you've been getting some magazines in the mail lately. We sent them. We're going to do a lot worse to you if you don't shape up.

How do you know this isn't a crank letter? Your name is John A. Smith. Look at the labels on the magazines you've been getting. They read John S., John T., John O., and John P. Smith. S.T.O.P. Get the meaning?"

The middle initial is only one of the authenticators that vigilantes can use to ensure that their communications will not be dismissed as crank calls or notes. Any simple detail that only the subject or the vigilante are likely to know will do. If the immediate harassing tactic used is to have merchandise delivered to the target's home, having pizzas delivered on the first evening, liquor on the second, and other types of food on the third will serve as an authenticator when mentioned in a letter or phone call.

Generally the vigilante will want to maintain a low profile and therefore will want to have as few law officers assigned to his case as possible, if any at all. The vigilante who sends a letter by mail may have the Postal Inspectors on his case, and although this is not a serious problem unless he is careless enough to put on a return address, it is a complication that he will want to avoid. Hand-delivering a letter eliminates this problem. A letter can easily be slipped under a door or dropped into the target's mailbox when he isn't looking. If the target works in a more or less public place it is easier yet — an envelope with his name on it will find its way to him, whether left on a table, desk or even on the floor.

Telephone calls are sometimes used but they are less productive, not because they can be traced, but because the call can degenerate into a shouting match if the target gets angry. The vigilante will in no event stay on the phone for very long, to avoid a trace, and this does not allow much time to effectively deliver a message if the target is unreceptive.

The signature on a warning letter is a simple thing but it can be a problem. Naturally the vigilante will not sign his name but a signature such as: "A former customer" can cause problems too. The simplest is often the best, and signing the letter; "The Vigilantes" will tell the target nothing except to imply that there is more than one through the use of the plural.

36. The Chain

Often a vigilante action starts with a little incident that might pass on in other circumstances and be forgotten. The vigilante, however, seizes upon it and exploits it to the fullest in the service of his cause.

A common example is that of the parent who finds his son using drugs. Many parents will try to deal with the situation by conventional methods, which usually mean exhorting the son to stop this dangerous habit, or taking him to a doctor, or in the last extreme, calling the police. These methods all have their place but they are all unsatisfying to the vigilante, who wants to see some positive action taken.

If the parent or a close relative is a vigilante, the chain starts there. He questions the son for the name and location of his source of supply. Many times drug users are reluctant to give this sort of information, particularly to the police, because they are afraid of reprisals. In this case the son can truthfully be assured that the source will never know who told on him and that any reprisals are out of the question.

The next link in the chain is the dealer who supplied the drugs to the son. The vigilante, alone or with some others, finds this source and interrogates him. The dealer may or may not be cooperative: there are ways of ensuring his cooperation in any case. If he is forthright he can be released and promised the same protection as was the son. As the vigilantes are not the police they obviously can keep the secret of the source of their information much better.

Once the dealer gives up the name and location of the wholesaler, the operation moves into high gear. That is when it will be decided whether to pursue this up the chain, or to simply terminate the wholesaler without any further ado.

The principle of working up the chain is fundamental: each criminal has at least one contact. The petty pusher in the street may not know the name of "Mr. Big" but he does know who his source of supply is. He can be made to talk. Then the next step is laid out with the identity of the wholesaler. He can be made to inform. The process must be taken step by step, which does take some time, but it can be done and done well, better than the police can do.

Vigilantes can do better at this than the police because of two reasons:

A) If a particular person is recalcitrant there are ways of making him talk that the police cannot or do not use.

B) The safety of informants can be doubly guaranteed because the vigilantes work in secret and they can terminate a particularly dangerous link in the chain, if necessary. In our first example, the vigilante can decide to liquidate the pusher to protect the son against reprisals.

Working up the chain is applicable to any sort of criminal enterprise at almost any time. A burglar caught in the act and taken alive can be "sweated" for the identity of his "fence". A car thief caught during a stakeout can be made to talk before he is disposed of.

37. Trashing - The Destruction Of Property

Often when vigilantes take action against a criminal or a group of criminals there is a certain amount of property involved. The criminal has to live somewhere; the stolen goods have to be stored somewhere. Sometimes the criminal gang operates out of a "legitimate" business as a "front". These all are vulnerable to destruction and the means chosen are as varied as the type of business involved.

A lot of nonsense has been written about means of physical destruction of property by people who are good at writing a sensational story but who are not familiar with the hard facts. A lot of attention has been devoted to exotic timers, explosives, and thermite bombs but in reality most destruction can be accomplished with just two things: fire and water. What determines the best one to use is the nature of the property and the availability of each one, as well as some special considerations.

There are two types of property to be considered: hard and soft. Hard property is a building containing machinery, building supplies, and items that are not very vulnerable to water damage. Soft property is paper, fiber, fabrics, cement, and other materials that are damaged or destroyed by drowning. There are many hybrid cases, such as the one a few years back when vigilantes did a "number" on a company that had cement trucks. One night the vigilantes stole into the yard and filled the tanks of the trucks with cement and water, mixed them thoroughly, and let the mixture set. After a few hours the trucks were effectively out of commission.

Water damage is slightly more difficult to arrange than setting a fire but it offers the outstanding advantage of being very unobtrusive. It is hard to set a fire and to burn a building to the ground without intervention by the fire department. Water damage is slow and silent, and the sophisticated vigilante will choose it whenever possible.

Every building has water outlets in it somewhere and the question is whether the water can be placed where it will do the most good. If there is a sprinkler system or a fire hose it is easy to turn it on and soak the entire area in a very short time. With sprinkler systems the outlets have a piece of metal holding the valve shut and this can be twisted off with pliers. Turning on a fire hose is as easy as turning a valve.

The advantage of using water is that the vigilante can remain on the scene for a long time, directing the streams of water where they will do the most good. The contents of closets and drawers are usually very vulnerable to water damage. Carpeting, furniture, and draperies are easily damaged. The effect of the water can be enhanced by chemicals, such as dyes, fertilizers, flour, starch, or cement added to the water or sprinkled on the wet area.

Paper and paper products are more vulnerable to water damage than they are to fire, as a rule. This is because packaged paper is tightly compressed and does not burn easily. Paper is always very absorbent, however, and the vigilante who wants to destroy a large amount of paper will drown it rather than burn it.

Fire is effective against anything that will burn, obviously, and also anything that can be damaged by heat, flame, or smoke. Restaurants, bars, retail stores, machine shops, warehouses, and many other types of premises are vulnerable.

The basic misconception about setting fires is a preoccupation with exotic timing devices. In reality they are used very rarely. If there is no time for the vigilantes to get away there probably is no time for the fire to do any damage before it is put out. In any event, the fire itself is what draws the attention of any witnesses, not the sight of men discreetly departing. Any vigilante who comes upon a witness after he has set the fire will tell the person to call the fire department, if he is cunning, rather than act in a furtive manner.

There are three components to setting a fire: the timer,

the igniter, and the fuel. Most of the time a timer is unnecessary but sometimes a couple of minutes, enough to get out of the building, can be obtained by the simple trick of a lit cigarette inserted into a book of matches, so that when the cigarette reaches the match heads a flame will result. Most of the time a trail of gasoline will serve the purpose equally well. It takes time for the flame to work its way down a long trail of gasoline and the trail can be laid to afford the vigilante a great degree of safety, if that is required.

The igniter is what sets off the rest of the material. Gasoline is a popular choice because it is so cheap and it is so easily available. It is possible to mix fuel oil with the gasoline for a higher caloric output but it is hardly worth the trouble because gasoline in its pure state is ideal for the job. In addition, the vigilante walking with a can of gasoline in his hand will not attract any attention. If the situation is such that a can of gasoline might cause some problems, the gasoline can be carried in another container, such as a cooking oil can.

The igniter is easy to set alight and it, in turn, lights the fuel, which is the main body of the combustible. Wood, bales of hay, motor oil, furniture, and many other substances will burn well once they are started on their way by a hot flame from the igniter. Often the combustibles are dispersed in piles or in different rooms, so that the arsonist will lay a trail of gasoline connecting them, rather than go around lighting each one while the fire blazes around him. For reasons of safety, it is better to be at the edge of the area when it goes up than in the middle.

The vigilante who has done his homework will know if the premises he is burning has a sprinkler system or not, and if there is one, he will know where the shut-off valve is located so that he can disable the sprinkler before starting. Sometimes the sprinkler is wired in to an alarm system and this must be dealt with too.

A special case is that of motors and machinery. The cliche in dealing with these is to suggest the use of a thermite bomb to damage them. In reality the powdered magnesium needed to make thermite must be bought somewhere and as it is not available in the local supermarket obtaining it can be a problem. Additionally, the chemical supply house which stocks it probably will notify the police of any purchases of this material, as it has little use apart from making incendiary devices.

Machinery can be damaged not only by the heat but by solder being placed at points where it will run down and clog the works as it melts. By contrast with magnesium, solder is plentiful and easy to obtain, no questions asked.

One aspect of arson that is rarely considered in fiction but is important in real life is controlling the spread of the fire. To a pathological arsonist, the bigger the better, but to a vigilante a controlled fire is critically important, for he does not want to hurt innocent people while punishing the guilty.

A detached building will often be ideal for arson because of the limitation on the spread of the fire. If the buildings are connected then there is a problem. It is more severe if the premises to be trashed are a suite of offices in a building with many other offices. Then it is almost impossible to start a fire that will not spread. The vigilante will consider each situation on its individual merits and decide on the best method of attack.

Possibly the most important aspect of arson is the question of insurance. The vigilante would find it counter-productive to destroy the criminal's property only to have the insurance company replace it with new and perhaps better property. Fortunately, most insurance policies will not pay off in case of arson. This makes the vigilante's task easier, for a while it may be desireable to make an assassination look like an accident, it will not be wise to make a fire look as if it started accidentally.

Fire investigators are quick to spot signs of arson, such as burn trails left by gasoline used to spread the fire from room to room. A couple of gasoline cans left lying around will complete the picture for even the densest investigator.

Sometimes, for various reasons, neither fire nor water are suitable for use. Then other, more time-consuming methods must be used to accomplish the destruction. A hammer and crowbar will be very useful, as they can be used to destroy almost anything. Sometimes even that amount of effort is more than is needed to accomplish the desired degree of destruction. For example, in the case of an attack on an unethical auto dealership, a can opener scraped along the side of each new car several times caused the dealer the expense of having each one refinished and repainted.

The timing of the attack is usually critical for two reasons: to avoid witnesses and to avoid injuring innocent people. It goes without saying that a vigilante does not want to burn up innocent people but it is also important to realize that some methods of destruction make a lot of noise. Nighttime or a weekend are the best times for an attack. A weekend is preferable if the method used is water, which takes time to soak in. If cement is used, the longer it has to set the better.

If the situation permits, a few extra items carried in on the attack will make a big difference in the results. A small sledgehammer, used to break the valve off a gas line, will be useful if fire is to be used. A sack of flour sprinkled on the floor will make any carpeting impossible to clean after it dries out. Starch or cement will do the same. Furniture and fabric can be attacked the same way. A few packets of permanent fabric dye will devastate any clothing, drapes, furniture, rolls of fabric, or carpeting. The advantage of these items for vigilantes is their easy availability and low cost. Exotic chemicals and devices make more interesting reading for the armchair commando, but the simple everyday items are what the vigilante uses.

38. The Risk Of Injury

It rarely happens that a vigilante is injured or killed in the line of "duty". Almost without exception, it is the target who suffers the injury. This has been true throughout the history of vigilantism and it is so for three reasons:

1) The vigilantes usually, if not always, have the advantage of surprise, catching the criminal unprepared.

2) The vigilantes usually outnumber the criminals, and that is a great advantage if it comes to a gunfight or a punchout.

3) The vigilantes take prudent protective measures in advance to minimize the risk to themselves. In a stakeout they pick positions with good cover and good fields of fire, for example.

With all that, there is still a slight risk of injury and the injury can be one which will be serious enough to compromise the group and its objective. Injuries can be broken down into three kinds:

A) Slight, which do not either cause much damage to the victim or pose any risk to the operation. This can include mild knife wounds, bullet grazes, and even getting the hand caught in a car door. The wound is slight enough to treat without professional help.

B) Moderate, which includes all wounds which require professional medical attention, except gunshot wounds. A broken arm can be explained away: so can a knife wound. These can be treated by a doctor without risk of compromising the vigilante group.

C) Severe, which includes all gunshot wounds and some knife wounds which cannot be explained away as accidents, such as multiple stabbings in the abdomen or in the back. A person going to the emergency ward for treatment cannot easily claim that he "shot himself shaving" or that he "fell on his knife seven times." It is customary, and in many locales it is required by law, to report all gunshot and felonious wounds to the police. This can cause the whole operation to become unglued.

The vigilante can take few precautions beyond the normal ones. There is little prospect of recruiting a doctor to the group for the purpose of getting clandestine treatment for such injuries. Doctors, for the most part, are primarily interested in personal profit and well-being, rather than practicing altruism or doing something to better their community. There are exceptions, of course, but most will not risk their privileged status by breaking the law. Even when the risk is slight, they simply don't want to be bothered.

If a member of the vigilante group is lucky enough to have a doctor in the family, or as a close friend, the chances are improved. In the rare instance where the doctor is himself a vigilante, the problem is mostly solved. The only difficulty remaining is that the injury may be so severe as to require hospitalization, an operating room, and intensive care facilities. Then the vigilantes have to improvise but the operation may still become unglued.

The improvisation usually consists of fudging the evidence and making the injured vigilante look like the victim of the crime. Many times, such as in a stakeout, the facts fit this explanation well, and the victim can be described as a passersby who was shot or stabbed by the criminal.

The same applies if one of the vigilantes is killed. The death can be made to look like the result of the felon's action and nothing else.

In all of these possibilities, the risk is there, and the vigilante learns to live with it. In fact, most of them accept the risk without much thought or soul-searching.

39. Vigilante "No-Nos"

There have been several cases of vigilantes either being made to look like fools or being prosecuted because they made severe errors in their operations. The major errors are as follows:

A) Abandoning secrecy or seeking publicity. It is obvious that anyone stepping forward to claim credit for killing a criminal under circumstances that are not strictly self-defense is likely to be charged with murder. Additionally, anyone who openly takes on the actions of a vigilante can expect to be stopped and harassed by the official police. Anyone who openly advocates vigilantism or who induces someone else to join him can be prosecuted for inciting violence, or worse. Even organizing any sort of group for the most defensive purposes can cause problems, as the Red Berets have found in New York. They have been subjected to personal attacks and vilification by city officials and arrest in some cases, despite the feeling among citizens and subway riders that they are doing some good. With their conspicuous uniforms they are a target for derision and slander.

B) Openly patrolling an area. Some years back two men were arrested for carrying shotguns in a swampy area a mile from Kennedy Airport in New York. Air Force One was expected to land momentarily and although the men were too far away to pose any threat to the President, their explanation that they were there to "protect the President" did not impress the authorities enough to prevent their being arrested.

C) Challenging law enforcement agencies on their own ground and trying to do their job for them. Recently the members of one ogranization announced that the Border

Patrol was not doing an adequate job of keeping out illegal aliens and that they were going to take up the task of patrolling the border to keep the aliens out. The authorities reacted in the usual manner and announced that anyone they caught trying to patrol the border would be arrested.

D) Joining a high-profile group or organization. There are various types of organizations appealing for members by advertising in newspapers and magazines. Some of these are outright scams which ask for membership dues, issue cards to the applicants, and do nothing else. There have been others that recruited in other ways but were too overt and quickly became known to the authorities and came under investigation. Prosecutions quickly followed and some of the leaders found themselves in jail.

One of the biggest weaknesses of such organizations is that they have known political ideals which inevitably means publicity, something that always hampers a vigilante. The police or other agencies obtain membership lists and they keep track of the members. Among the suspects in any investigation of vigilante actions would be the members of such organizations.

Some of the organizations are simply not serious. A hypothetical example would be one calling itself "The National Vigilante Association", and advertising in magazines, offering a "genuine Vigilante badge" and an identification card, a whistle, and a secret decoder ring. There might be a monthly magazine or newsletter and even a meeting or two but a group would necessarily be utterly ineffective, for everything they do is laid out in public and they would be under strict surveillance by the authorities.

Anyone who joined such an organization under the misguided belief that he was thereby doing something to help law and order would be about as effective as a child who got a badge out of a cereal box.

40. The Final Problem

Through the years vigilantes have performed many brave acts, taken many risks, and ended the careers of many dangerous criminals. They have stood up for their fellow citizens in the hour of maximum danger and greatest need. Yet, much of the honor that is rightfully theirs has not been awarded and an ungrateful public and jealous officials are only part of the reason.

It has happened that some vigilantes got intoxicated with their power. Some simply got carried away, liquidating first one criminal, then another, and another, and yet more, in a never-ending series. When they ran out of felons they started in on minor offenders, and then retrogressed to purging people who were not lawbreakers at all, in the strict sense of the word. In some cases they lashed out at wife-beaters and drunks.

It was in cases of these excesses that a new type of organization sprang up in the footsteps of the regulators and vigilantes; the moderators. These were other citizens who felt that the regulators had gone too far and had to be controlled, or moderated. It is unfortunate that this was necessary, for the struggles that resulted caused the deaths of many good men.

It is a temptation for any vigilante, once he gets a taste of action and realizes how easy it is to enforce the law in that way, to decide to try to correct other problems too and to try to enforce not only the law but mores and his own personal standards.

Killing gets easier all the time. After the first execution the vigilante finds the second one easier, and same with the third. While pitched gun battles do not get easier, and in fact may get harder, executions are less jarring after the vigilante has had a little experience under his belt. It becomes easier to tie the hangman's knot, to put that final bullet into the brain. More importantly, it becomes easier to imagine oneself as the sole defender of society, the lone upholder of law and order.

That is why it is critically important for the vigilantes to have good judgment and to know when to stop. More to the point, it is important to know where to stop. Enforcing the laws against serious crimes can degenerate into enforcing minor ones. It is silly to try to use vigilante tactics to punish people who beat their wives or spit on the sidewalk, yet sometimes it has come to that. For the vigilante, there is no shortage of important targets. We have a lot of criminals in this country, more than the police can handle. Moreover, there are more than any vigilantes existing today can handle. Even if the vigilantes executed fifty hardened felons per month throughout the country they would never run out of "business".

PART III.
SPECIAL PROBLEMS -
SPECIAL TECHNIQUES

41. The Crash Car

Vigilantes not only commit felonies in enforcing the law: they must often borrow directly from criminals' techniques to carry out their tasks. They must post a lookout during some of their actions; they must use stolen or spurious cars, and they must use ways of avoiding the police in exactly the same way that criminals do.

Avoiding the police is particularly important for the vigilante. The criminal may be resigned to shooting any policeman who gets in the way: some brutal killers might even be eager to do so. The vigilante cannot: he upholds the law in the end and killing a policeman is as disagreeable to him as is killing an innocent person. Therefore, as any contact with the police during an action would mean submitting to arrest, it is of critical importance for the vigilante to avoid that contact altogether.

One simple technique of avoiding contact when engaging in an action is the spurious phone call. A call to a location several blocks away will ensure that the patrol car assigned to the sector will not be on hand when the vigilantes strike. This is permissible when the action is arson, for example, and the evidence is hard or undesireable to conceal. In the event of an assassination that is to look like a mugging or an accident, however, a spurious phone call would be a clue to the police that the case is more involved than at first sight.

It is for this reason, and for a backup, that the crash car technique is sometimes used. An individual who does not otherwise work in the operation is assigned the task of driving around the area in his own car, carrying full identification and the documents for the car. He or she has the disagreeable task of ramming any police car that they see heading for the

187

scene of the action. The collision is a low-speed one, usually a rear-ender, as they are easier to control and minimize the chances of injury. The driver stops immediately after the crash, apologizes, and offers the explanation that he or she sneezed and lost control of the car momentarily. This explanation is always credible and will avoid the more severe complications, such as being arrested for criminal negligence.

It is essential that the car and its driver be completely legitimate and capable of withstanding investigation, because that is their function; to stand there being investigated and tying up the police car and its crew while doing so.

The liability will be on the driver of the crash car, and as this will cover damage to the police vehicle as well as to the crash car itself, the money involved can be substantial. It means a serious financial sacrifice, as the least that can happen is that the insurance rates will go up, and a severe test of the dedication of the vigilante.

The role of crash car driver is a perfect example of the hard edge of the reality of being a vigilante today. Those who have romantic ideas about gun battles with desperate felons will be disappointed by the dull and prosaic, though essential, role of the crash car driver. It takes a particularly sincere member of a vigilante group to volunteer for such a part.

42. Mercury

The vigilante's resources are very limited and the crime problem is very large. While it would be ideal to shoot each and every member of organized crime, or to inject him with a dose of cyanide, it simply isn't possible. Most vigilantes can't make a significant dent in the crime problem using conventional methods. Some of the more imaginative ones are using mercury to do the job.

The use of mercury is worthwhile when it is not possible to dispose of the target in any conventional manner for a variety of reasons. The target may simply be too well protected, or the logistics of the strike may be too difficult to arrange.

Mercury is a heavy metal, liquid at room temperature. It is poisonous when its vapor is inhaled. The advantages over other poisons are many:

A) It is commonly available in fever thermometers which can be bought in any drugstore or supermarket without signing for them. This avoids the paperwork tail that is the result of buying other poisons.

B) It is easy to use and to deliver, as close contact with the target or his food is not required. A few drops in the carpet of a room he frequents is enough. A bedroom is fine and an office will do.

C) Mercury is not dangerous to the user, as contact with it for a short period of time is harmless to most people. It can be carried without danger.

D) Possession is not grounds for either arrest or even suspicion. A thermometer is a harmless appearing object and even a physical search will turn up nothing incriminating.

E) Delivery can even be made to look like an accident if there are people in the room. Dropping and breaking a thermometer is not an event that will cause any excitement.

The only disadvantage is that the effects are slow to appear. Mercury poisoning is not even necessarily deadly but may be merely debilitating if the target is removed from the source.

Breathing the vapor over a period of time causes a feeling of listlessness and a loss of apetite. There is weight loss. At this point the person may go to see a doctor, who might put him into the hospital, where he will most likely start to recover, being removed from the poison. Death is unlikely. When the person has recovered enough, he may go back to work, where the cycle will start over if the poison is in his office.

Innocent people are not greatly endangered. Visitors will not breathe enough of the vapor to succumb.

The effect of this technique is gradual and cumulative, not as dramatic as a raid or a shootout, but effective in the long run. The people who are regularly on the premises of a warehouse used for the storage and distribution of stolen property, for example, will be far less effective at their dishonest jobs if they are coming down with chronic mercury poisoning.

It is possible for a diagnosis of mercury poisoning to be made by a doctor, but finding the actual cause is almost impossible. In any event, if the target relocates it is always possible to deliver some more to the new address.

43. Disposal Of Bodies

The vigilante must sometimes borrow gangster methods and some of them pertain to disposal of corpses. Getting rid of a body can be important to a vigilante for two reasons; the continuation of secrecy and disposal of the evidence. A vigilante does not want to advertise and sometimes leaving a corpse is too blatant. It may not be possible to make the death look accidental or the result of a robbery. In that case the last thing a vigilante would like to see is a corpse telling its silent story to the police and other interested parties.

Evidence is essential to a prosecution. Without the evidence there is no case. Better yet, without a body or any indication of foul play the case will be written up as another missing person. This can be very convenient for the vigilante. A criminal who is executed in secret and buried in an isolated spot will perhaps be missed by his friends, family, or associates, but there will be nothing to indicate that he did not simply have a lapse of memory and wander off into the vast nether-land of this country, under another name and with another personality.

There are basically four ways that gangsters use to dispose of corpses:

A) Burial. This can be accomplished in many ways. The simplest is to take the body out to an isolated spot, dig a hole, and dump him in. Some try to save a little trouble by taking the condemned out alive, but sooner or later the candidate for death will realize that he is being taken for a "ride" and may well put up a fierce resistance. Therefore it is better in the long run to have already cancelled his birth certificate before starting out on the journey.

The choice of burial grounds is wide and there are a lot of

opportunities. A place in the wilds can be chosen. A more close-in place would be a landfill, where the site will be built upon in the near future. An isolated cave can be used as a repository but it is essential that the entrance be closed off so that the body is not found by hikers or explorers.

If the choice is simple burial, a common mistake is to make the hole too shallow. If that is the case a wild dog or other animal, smelling the rotting flesh, may dig up the body or a part of it to get a meal. This increases the chances of discovery. The concensus is that six feet is an ideal depth for a grave. No less offers any security.

B) Immersion. This can be "burial at sea" or just in a river or a lake. Whatever the case, gangsters are often embarrassed by the body coming to the surface again to advertise the crime. This is because the tissues, and particularly the contents of the intestines, release gas which makes the body come to the surface after a week or two, resulting in the "floaters" which dot our waterways. Weighting a body down is no guarantee that it will not come to the surface sooner or later. Only piercing the abdomen will give any chance of success, as it allows the gas to escape. Even this does not work all the time and only completely gutting the body will give any assurance that the weights tied to it will keep it down. Fifty pounds of iron or cement blocks will ensure that the body stays down if there is no intestinal gas to float it back up.

C) Entombment. Owning a construction company is doubly useful for organized crime — they can use the company as a "front" in the conventional manner and they can get rid of the bodies by burying them in the foundations of buildings being put up. This method is a particularly suitable way of getting rid of a body so that it will not be discovered by accident.

Usually it is the footing of a large building that is the most suitable, as the body is covered by hundreds of tons of concrete rather than just a few hundred pounds, as would be the case in a private house, and the life of a large building is at least twice as long as that of a house, making it that much longer before demolition and disentombment. Similarly, the bedding of a superhighway is less likely to be disturbed than the subsurface of a city street, as streets are being dug up constantly for the placement of new pipes and electrical conduits.

Above-ground entombment is a practice that comes to us from Europe, in fact, the French verb ENMURER means exactly that: walling up a person, dead or alive. Wherever there are thick walls, thick enough to contain a body, this is a possibility. Of course, most modern houses and buildings are made with walls that are far too thin for this sort of use but there are still some constructions that can be made to serve this purpose. Dams are typically built with walls that are yards thick, even the small ones. Modern buildings with several sub-basements are ideal, as a hole can easily be cut in the outer wall and the body buried from underground, as it were.

D) Incineration. Burning the body is a very efficient way of ensuring that the evidence does not turn up at an inconvenient moment later on. It is not necessary to own a crematorium to do this. In some rare cases a fire can be built in a remote spot and the body cremated but it is usually more feasible to use facilities that are close to town. In some locales garbage is routinely incinerated and the body can be crammed in with the garbage, although it requires some stamina to cut the body up into conveniently sized pieces for this.

Many industrial processes use extreme heat and huge furnaces and acces to them is the only problem. A soap vat or a steel furnace will destroy a body completely enough for either the gangster's or the vigilante's purposes. Bakers' ovens are not hot enough and the smell would attract attention: the same goes for the ovens in metal heat treatment plants. On the other hand a foundry has ovens that will develop the couple of thousand degrees needed to do an effective job of destroying a body.

There are many other ways of disposing of an inconvenient corpse but they depend so much on special circumstances that they are of little practical use. An undertaker or his employee might include an extra passenger in a coffin, and someone with access to a pet food plant might arrange to feed the unwanted visitor to the kitty-cats.

Whatever the method chosen, the only requirement is that it work one hundred per cent.

44. The Wrong Man

It often happens that bodies are found stuffed into the trunk of a car or in some lonely spot. Many times these are the result of a vigilante action. What is not generally known is that sometimes the police investigation results in the arrest of an innocent person. Every homicide is investigated, however superficially, and sometimes the superficiality of the investigation is the cause of the wrongful accusation. Other times someone happens to be in the wrong place at the wrong time. More often it is because the person killed has many enemies. One can expect this from a criminal. If one of his enemies does not have an alibi, he might well be arrested by the police, and the evidence manipulated to fit their suspicions. While this is not exactly "framing" it is close enough.

A vigilante is on the side of law and order, and it makes him acutely uncomfortable to see someone charged with a crime that he did not commit. Yet, almost nothing can be done to minimize this danger, as there is no way of predicting what the police will do or what their investigation will turn up. Most of all, there is no way to predict luck, good or bad.

There is a method of dealing with the situation if it arises, and a simple precaution to almost assure the release of the wrong man if he is arrested. This involves the use of an authenticator.

When the police investigate a homicide they do not release all of their information to the public or the press. They hold back certain details that only the guilty party would know, for example, how many shots hit the victim, or where he was stabbed, the contents of his pockets, or any bizarre details if it is a sex crime. That way they have a way of authenticating a confession.

Whenever a crime is committed there may be false suspects. Some are the bizarre "confessors" to be found on the fringes of society, people who have a psychological quirk that makes them go to the police and to confess to crimes that they did not commit. These can be quickly screened out by asking them about details that they could not know if they were innocent. Other suspects can be eliminated in the same way, if the police are conscientious.

The vigilante who wants to take a precaution against the wrong man being accused will leave an authenticator with the body. This can be anything at all, any detail that is likely to be noted by the police. If he leaves the victim's wallet, he can make a list of everything in it. He can leave a token, such as a rabbit's foot, something that will not seem unusual to the policemen searching the body but yet will be noted on an inventory list. It should not be of any great value, as there are still some dishonest policemen who would slip it into their pockets and let it be believed that it was stolen from the victim by the murderer.

If the wrong man is arrested, and if the police do not immediately discover their error, the vigilante sends them a note, using a rented typewriter and handling the paper and envelope with gloves. He mentions the authenticator and confesses anonymously. Such a note might go like this:

"Dear Inspector——;
You have arrested the wrong man for the murder of ——. He did not do it: I did. When I killed ——, I took the handkerchief from his jacket pocket and put it in his right rear pants pocket. I took his tie off and put it in his right hand. I put a handful of gravel in his left jacket pocket. I had my own reasons for killing —— and I will not tell you what they are, as I don't want to be identified, but I assure you that you have the wrong man in custody."

Appendix A
Surveillance

SURVEILLANCE

The following is a copy of an actual surveillance work-sheet used by a private detective agency on a job and taken from information provided by the police. The names and locations have been changed. Note the similarity to the descriptions of stakeouts given earlier:

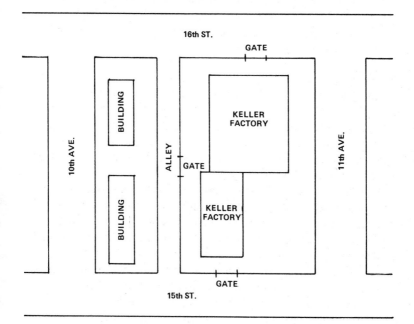

Surveillance of the Keller factory, 1005 North 15th St. John Smith, 27, 6' 1", 200 lbs. a recently discharged employee, has made threatening statements that he would damage the equipment.

The objective of the surveillance is to watch all three gates to the plant, which is open 24 hours a day, and to keep a log of all people and vehicles going in or out, and to watch for John Smith. BE DISCREET. Park your car far enough away from the factory so that you won't be seen by anyone coming in or going out. Record all plate numbers and descriptions. If Smith is seen, keep as close a watch on him as you can without being seen yourself. If he starts to do any damage to the company's property, phone the police. The nearest public phone is at the corner of 15th St. and 9th Ave. a block South of the plant.

After calling the police, call Fred Jones, 123-4567, or if you cannot get him, call James Johnson, 456-7890.

Smith is a Vietnam veteran and has a record of violence. Do not try to apprehend him yourself. Call the police.

In analyzing this surveillance, several things are worth some comment:

A) The text of the worksheet states explicitly that the operatives are not to try to apprehend the suspect but rather to call the police. This is often the pattern. The citizens' powers of arrest are very limited. Added to this is the fact that the operatives are not Commando types but older family men and that the rate of pay is six dollars per hour, not enough money to justify any risks.

B) The detective agency assigned two operatives to this task for each shift, not nearly enough to do a thorough job of watching all of the entrances. This is typical of anything run for profit. Actually, considering the layout of the plant and its surroundings, three men would be a more realistic number because the gates on three sides of the factory, the buildings obstructing the view, and the need to watch the fence on the fourth side is just too much for two men to handle.

C) The operatives were armed, not because they seriously considered that they were in any danger, but because the local laws permitted carrying sidearms. In any event, their instructions were to avoid direct contact with the suspect and to call the police.

Appendix B
A Quick Look At Guns

A QUICK LOOK AT GUNS

All sorts of firearms have been used with success in vigilante actions, from the flintlocks of pre-revolutionary days to the most modern rifles and pistols. Generally the firearms used have been the ones available rather than guns especially procured for the task.

With the gun culture prevalent in this country today it is easy for the vigilante or would-be vigilante to be misled into getting himself a veritable arsenal when something simpler will be perfectly adequate. A number of myths have arisen and become popularised in the gun magazines and their net result has been to arouse interest in certain types of guns and to stimulate sales.

One is the myth of the pistol, or more properly the mystique. Tons of paper have been devoted to the question of which pistol, in what caliber, is suitable for "combat" use. As there are many types of pistols and they are made in many calibers there is a lot of room for discussion. Dozens of articles have been written by the devotees of the automatic pistol, many others by the advocates of the revolver, etc. Opinions are many and the facts are stated in a misleading way on all sides.

Whatever the weapon used, the skill of the user is far more important than the type of weapon. A person who decides to buy a .45 automatic because he read in a magazine that it is a powerful pistol with enough "stopping power" to put down an assailant may find that he cannot shoot as well with that pistol as he can with his .22 rifle. Certain weapons fit certain people best. To try to use a weapon because a certain "expert" recommends it is a waste of time.

A pistol's main advantage is concealability. For the

vigilante this will be meaningful only in situations where there is no alternative to concealing a weapon on the person. In many stakeout and decoy operations, for example, a shotgun or rifle can be used with greater effect as there is no need to carry the weapon concealed. Generally speaking, the more powerful the weapon the better.

Pistols are also featured prominently in motion pictures, television programs, and "combat" matches. This can mislead many people into believing that the pistol is the best choice in many situations where something else would be better.

There is a certain "macho" image connected with a pistol which has largely to do with the glamorous treatment the pistol gets in the media. In reality the pistol is made for a certain purpose and to try to use it beyond its limits is to invite trouble. It is a short-range, easily hidden weapon of limited power. That's it.

If a pistol is necessary for a certain action, it is important to choose the right type. Each type has its advocates and it is easy to become confused. In a shootout, the right type is the one that does the job in the hand of the person using it. It has to be a pistol that feels comfortable, fits the hand, does not recoil beyond the ability of the shooter to tolerate, and accurate and powerful enough to kill or disable the target at the range at which it will be fired. It should be reliable.

Some advocate the Government Model .45 auto pistol as being the ideal pistol because it is prominent at matches. A match is not a gunfight and a pistol designed for winning a match is not necessarily the best for use in a situation where the shooter is shooting for real. Moreover, the pistols used in matches are specially tuned and have accessories, such as target sights, which impairs their concealability. Often their size makes them difficult to slip in and out of a pocket. A vigilante may not have any fancy gun leather as do the contestants in a match, and in any event few match holsters are designed for concealment.

Accuracy of the weapon is always related to the question: "Accurate enough for what?" Most pistols are inherently accurate enough to hit a man-sized target at a range of ten or twenty yards: many can do better than this. Performance

VIGILANTE HANDBOOK

will vary with the individual shooter. Not everyone is equally skilled and not everyone will find every gun fitting his hand equally well. Some guns are more comfortable to use than others, to some people.

Anyone who expects to have to shoot for real will do well to try his skill against cardboard man-sized targets first to find out what he can hit at what range. He will also have to be aware that many gunfights occur in the hours of darkness and that this will have a great effect on accuracy.

"Stopping power" is another subject that is the cause of many tons of paper being used. There are all sorts of opinions and mathematical-seeming "formulas" purporting to give a value of stopping power for various cartridges and weapons. All of these ignore two basic facts:

A) The effect of a bullet depends more on where it hits than any other factor.

B) Unlike the formulas, gunfights usually involve more than one bullet. This means that if the first shot doesn't do the job there are more in the gun, waiting to be fired. For the vigilante who is firing from behind cover, it doesn't matter very much if his opponent takes one second or two or three to go down. In any event, no hand weapon, no matter what the supposed "stopping power" guarantees either a one shot kill or immediate disablement. This directly contradicts what some gun writers claim but it is what happens out in the field.

Some popular weapons for use in vigilante actions are given here. Each has its place; each has its followers and critics. None is suitable for every situation. The final choice is up to the vigilante who will actually be using the weapon.

PISTOLS:

.38 caliber Smith & Wesson Chief, for concealability.

.357 Ruger Security-Six, for more power, longer range, at some sacrifice in concealability.

9mm Browning Hi-Power or Smith & Wesson Model 39 for a flat, easily carried automatic.

RIFLES:

.223 Ruger Mini-14, for a light, carbine-size weapon that has adequate range and power and a large ammunition capacity.

Remington Model 788 in Cal. .308 for a more powerful weapon with longer range, suitable for sniping use when fitted with a good scope.

SHOTGUNS:

12 gauge Remington, Ithaca, Mossberg pump-action shotguns.

These all have a reputation for reliability and safety, and can be bought either in long barrel length or with shorter barrels for compactness. Most shotguns have easily changed barrels so that one barrel can be cut down and another, in original state, be used to replace it after the action is over.

Appendix C
Body Armor - A Very Special Case

BODY ARMOR — A VERY SPECIAL CASE

It is a little known and unpublicised fact that at least half of the policemen in this country wear some sort of body armor routinely while on duty. This is particularly true of officers on patrol duty, where danger may present itself suddenly. Administrative personnel and detectives rarely do. Special units, such as the armed teams which go under the name of SWAT, or something similar, always do. They wear extra-heavy armor sometimes known as "flak jackets".

The officer on patrol, however, cannot be encumbered with heavy equipment. He must have something that he can tolerate for at least an eight-hour shift. There are light vests available that are made of ballistic cloth and weigh about three pounds.

The officer working as a decoy or on stakeout duty will also be armored. In his case the vital factor is not so much comfort but compatibility with civilian clothes. If the officer working stakeout is doing so from a concealed position he can wear a flak jacket or even a suit of armor, but if he is in sight he must be concerned about his appearance.

The decoy is always armored with a light ballistic vest as he is typically in the position of greatest danger. As decoy duty does not usually last as long as a shift spent on patrol, comfort is less important and the decoy can well tolerate such a vest even in the hottest climates, knowing that it may well save his life in the next few hours.

So it goes with the vigilante too. While the vigilante does not expose himself to as much risk as the policeman, in most cases, if he is mounting a decoy operation the danger is equally great.

Procuring body armor may cause some difficulties. While there are no laws governing the sale or possession of body armor some manufacturers will not sell to civilians. Again, some will. If one of the vigilantes is a policeman, the difficulties can be overcome. Body armor can also be bought by mail. This is made easy by the fact that due to its design, a close or accurate fit is not critical.

There are different levels of protection available, with the more sturdy vests being heavier. For the vigilante, who does not have to wear it for endless hours on patrol, the heavier vest is tolerable.

In many cities uniform shops catering to policemen stock these vests and the vigilante can go in and try them on to determine how well he can wear one. While fit is not critical and neither is weight, in his case, compatibility with clothing is, and a vest that is so bulky that it cannot be worn under a shirt in a hot climate would be useless. In cooler climates, the vest can be worn instead of a shirt, undershirt, or sweater, under the coat.

Outer clothing will give some protection against knife wounds, another fact that is not immediately obvious. A ballistic vest, on the other hand, is more vulnerable to penetration by a knife than by a bullet, because the blade is sharp and tends to cut the fibers. A bullet tends to just batter its way through. Additional protection can be improvised, such as a sheet of metal worn on top of the vest, if climate and clothing permit.